TWENTIETH CENTURY
INTERPRETATIONS

MAYNARD MACK, *Series Editor*
Yale University

NOW AVAILABLE
Collections of Critical Essays
ON

ADVENTURES OF HUCKLEBERRY FINN

ALL FOR LOVE

ARROWSMITH

AS YOU LIKE IT

THE DUCHESS OF MALFI

THE FROGS

THE GREAT GATSBY

HAMLET

HENRY V

THE ICEMAN COMETH

SAMSON AGONISTES

THE SCARLET LETTER

THE SOUND AND THE FURY

TWELFTH NIGHT

WALDEN

THE WASTE LAND

TWENTIETH CENTURY INTERPRETATIONS
OF
THE SCARLET LETTER

TWENTIETH CENTURY INTERPRETATIONS
OF

THE SCARLET LETTER

A Collection of Critical Essays

Edited by
JOHN C. GERBER

Prentice-Hall, Inc. A SPECTRUM BOOK *Englewood Cliffs, N.J.*

Current printing (last number):
10 9 8 7 6 5 4 3 2 1

Contents

vii

PART THREE—*Techniques*

PART FOUR—*Interpretations*

Introduction

by John C. Gerber

For a man who was one of the shrewdest observers of the human condition, Nathaniel Hawthorne had a surprisingly uneventful life. Unlike Herman Melville and Mark Twain he traveled little—at least until he was about fifty—and unlike Poe he was never driven by imminent disaster. What is obvious is that he was a man of great sensitivity who found largely in reading and contemplation the inspiration and material that he needed for his writing.

Born in Salem, Massachusetts, on July 4, 1804, he was the second of three children and the only son of Nathaniel and Elizabeth Manning Hathorne (Hawthorne himself added the "w" to the name). His family on both sides had come over from England in the seventeenth century, and with the growth of the town had become prosperous and influential citizens. Of William Hathorne, who arrived in 1630, Hawthorne wrote, "The figure of that first ancestor, invested by family tradition with a dim and dusky grandeur, was present to my boyish imagination as far back as I can remember it. It still haunts me, and induces a sort of home-feeling with the past." The "home-feeling" must have been a mixed one, however, since William Hathorne was remembered in histories not only as a soldier and magistrate but also as the judge who had sentenced a Quaker woman to be whipped at the tail of a cart through the streets of Salem, Boston, and Dedham. As if this were not enough, William's son John had been one of the three judges who condemned fellow townsmen to death in the infamous Salem witchcraft trials of 1692. One of the so-called witches had pronounced a curse on another of the three judges—"God will give you blood to drink"—but the event looms so importantly in the writings of Hawthorne that it would seem as though he felt his own family forever accursed. His mother's family—the Mannings—arrived in America in 1679. Chiefly artisans and businessmen, their history was less eventful than that of the Hathornes, but they played a larger role in the life of the young Nathaniel since it was his uncle Robert Manning who took care of him and his mother and sisters after his father died in 1808 in Surinam, Dutch Guiana.

Although Hawthorne was strong and well-built, his boyhood was less

active than most. On the death of his father, his mother retired into
her room and became a semi-recluse for the remainder of her long life.
The home thus became abnormally quiet for a young boy. It became
even more quiet when Hawthorne developed a lameness playing ball
that required three years to wear off. During this time reading had to
substitute largely for physical activity. In 1818 the Hawthornes moved
to Raymond, Maine, where Hawthorne was later to say he contracted
his "cursed habit of solitude." But he was back in Salem the next year
studying in Samuel Archer's school and working in the office of his
uncle's stagecoach company. By 1821 he was ready for college, and in
October of that year he enrolled as a freshman at Bowdoin in Brunswick, Maine.

The most significant event of his four college years was his decision
to become a writer. In a characteristically bantering manner, he wrote
to his mother, "I do not want to be a doctor and live by men's diseases,
nor a minister to live by their sins, nor a lawyer and live by their quar-
rels. So, I don't see that there is anything left for me but to be an
author." So far as college itself was concerned, he seems to have read
widely and to have distinguished himself in composition. But he
possessed an independent spirit and more often than not remained
aloof from college activities. He was graduated eighteenth in a class
of thirty-eight. His best friends at Bowdoin were Horatio Bridge,
Franklin Pierce, and Jonathan Cilley, all of whom were to help him
later with publishers or political appointment. Henry Wadsworth
Longfellow, another classmate, would later review his *Twice-Told
Tales* so warmly that Hawthorne's reputation began to spread beyond
the limits of New England.

The next twelve years, 1825-1837, Hawthorne spent principally in
the seclusion of his "chamber under the eaves" in his mother's house
in Salem. He himself later said that not more than a score in Salem
in those years were aware of his existence. Yet it would be a mistake
to think of him as a misanthrope or even a recluse. He got out of the
house for long walks and trips to the library, and in the summers he
ventured as far as Maine and Niagara Falls. His letters during the
period indicate that while he was increasingly the skeptic, he was not
depressed. Nevertheless it is true that he was alone most of the time.
Chiefly he read and wrote. During the twelve years almost twelve
hundred books at the Salem Athenaeum were charged out to the
Hawthornes, most of them undoubtedly meant for Nathaniel. A typical day found him writing in the morning and afternoon, and reading
in the evening.

Before the twelve years were out his writing had improved so mark-
edly that he was turning out tales that still remain some of the best
in the language. It was a training period in which he was both instruc-

tor and student. His first work, *Fanshawe* (1828), may have been started while he was at Bowdoin, which provides the locale for the story. It was a short imitation Gothic novel that was so inexpertly done that Hawthorne himself tried to buy up and destroy every copy he could lay hands on. He was dissatisfied with his next major effort too, a collection of stories he called *Seven Tales of My Native Land.* In a fit of exasperation he threw the manuscript into the fire, though by some happenstance two stories that were apparently part of the collection have survived, "Alice Doane's Appeal" and "The Hollow of the Three Hills." The latter he sent to the Salem *Gazette* where it appeared anonymously in 1830. From then on his tales and sketches appeared frequently—and anonymously—in New England newspapers and magazines until 1837 when he collected them as *Twice-Told Tales* and had them published with his name attached. By the time he was willing to leave his room under the eaves, he had developed a style that was unique among American writers for its dignity and intensity.

Between 1838 and 1842 Hawthorne wrote considerably less since he had fallen in love and needed to make more money than he could expect from his writing. The girl was Sophia Peabody, the semi-invalid daughter of a Salem dentist and the sister of Elizabeth Peabody, a noted feminist and reformer, and of Mary Peabody, who married the educator Horace Mann. Thanks to friends in the Democratic Party, Hawthorne obtained a position as measurer in the Boston Custom House. He held the job for two years, resigning in 1840 just before the newly elected Whig administration had a chance to throw him out. In April of 1841 he joined the Transcendentalists at Brook Farm, although he was interested more in finding a place where he and Sophia might live than in the Utopian dreams of the Transcendentalists. Unhappily the experience did not turn out as he had hoped, and he left Brook Farm in the fall of 1841. Ultimately, though, he was able to make use of the Farm as the setting for *The Blithedale Romance.*

Despite their unpromising future, Hawthorne and Sophia Peabody were married July 9, 1842. For income they had only the promise of payment for whatever he might write. He set to work with enthusiasm, however, and brought out the tales now to be found chiefly in *Mosses from an Old Manse* (the Hawthornes were living in the Old Manse at Concord) and some minor works, especially stories for children. But such writings did not bring in enough income for the family, especially after Una was born, and again Hawthorne sought out his friends for a political position. This time they responded by persuading President Polk to appoint him Surveyor at the Salem Custom House. He began his duties in April of 1846, and left in the summer of 1849 when he was forced out of office by the new Whig administration of Zachary Taylor. Angered and yet eager to return to writing, he began *The*

Scarlet Letter almost immediately and wrote so rapidly that the book was finished by February of 1850.

Although *The Scarlet Letter* brought Hawthorne considerable fame and some money, the family had to move from Salem to Western Massachusetts where they could live more economically. They settled in the summer of 1850 in the Red House at Lenox, only a few miles from Pittsfield where Herman Melville was living. The visits between the two men were enormously important for American literature, for Melville may well have decided to rewrite *Moby-Dick* as a result of his talks with Hawthorne. For Hawthorne the period was one of prodigious output. In 1851 he published *The House of the Seven Gables, The Snow Image and Other Twice-Told Tales,* and *True Stories from History and Biography*; in 1852 these were followed by *The Blithedale Romance, A Wonder-Book for Girls and Boys,* and a campaign biography of Franklin Pierce. The last was particularly important for the Hawthorne pocketbook since Pierce, after being elected in 1852, appointed Hawthorne to the most lucrative position he could, the consulship in Liverpool.

As consul Hawthorne had little time to write, but almost immediately after resigning in 1856 he began *The Ancestral Footstep*, which he never completed, and *The Marble Faun*, which he composed in Italy and England and published in 1860. The Hawthornes returned to the United States in 1860 where they settled down in Concord at "The Wayside." In the next few years Hawthorne wrote *Our Old Home* and started but failed to complete *Septimius Felton, Dr. Grimshawe's Secret,* and *The Dolliver Romance*. By the fall of 1863 his health began to fail—his precise illness has never been known—and in May of 1864 he died while on a trip for his health in the White Mountains with his old friend Franklin Pierce. He was buried in the Sleepy Hollow Cemetery in Concord. He was survived by his wife and three children, Una, Julian, and Rose.

II *The Writing of* The Scarlet Letter

Hawthorne had a right to feel bitter about being fired from his post as Surveyor of the Boston Custom House. To be sure, he had been appointed to the position by President Polk, a Democrat. But when Zachary Taylor, a Whig, was elected in 1848, he announced that proscription for party reasons was to cease. And certainly Hawthorne, the mildest of partisans, would seem to have had nothing to fear. But a group of Salem Whigs headed by Charles W. Upham, formerly pastor of the First Church of Salem, had other ideas. Defeated at first in their attempts to have Hawthorne removed, they charged him in

Washington with "corruption, iniquity, and fraud," and finally succeeded in having him replaced in July of 1849. The charges, of course, were wholly false—as newspapers throughout the country made clear. Indeed, the whole affair became a *cause célèbre*. Willam Cullen Bryant, for example, wrote in the New York *Evening Post* that Hawthorne's removal "was an act of wanton and unmitigated oppression" and "a gross breach of public faith on the part of the President." Long afterward Hawthorne could realize that being fired made his name known throughout the country as his tales never could have done. Moreover, the person of Upham gave him material for "The Custom House" and for the character of Judge Pyncheon in *The House of the Seven Gables*. But at the time he was hurt and angry.

Hawthorne had many a reason for turning back to writing. He had not been able to write while working as Surveyor, although he had been dallying with the idea of another volume of tales and sketches which he meant to call *Old-Time Legends: Together with Sketches, Experimental and Ideal,* and was eager to get started on it. More than that, the family badly needed money. There were two children now, and Hawthorne's mother, critically ill and dying, was living with the family. As if all this were not incentive enough, there was the driving desire to prove himself in the eyes of his many loyal friends. It is no great surprise, therefore, that Sophia could presently say that Hawthorne was writing "immensely."

Few writers have been better prepared for the task of composition. For years Hawthorne had been steeping himself in the history of early New England, not only in its events but, more importantly, in its customs, values, and ideas. His notebooks and journals were replete with ideas and details for stories, such as one entered in 1847: "A story of the effects of revenge, in diabolizing him who indulges in it." Maybe most important of all, he had learned in his tales and sketches how to project his ideas through character and symbol. In "The Gentle Boy," for example, he had dealt with the hostility of the Puritans to a creature of the affections, in "Young Goodman Brown" with the ambiguity of sin, in "The Minister's Black Veil" with the effects of an outer symbol of inner guilt, in "Rappaccini's Daughter" and "The Birthmark" with the man of intellect who is willing to sacrifice a loved one for the sake of learning, and in "Ethan Brand" with various combinations of the relation between head and heart. In "Endicott and the Red Cross" he had even given passing mention to a character who was eventually to become Hester Prynne. In short, he had experimented sufficiently with the dramatization of moral and psychological dilemmas to begin another such dramatization feeling sure of his powers.

He began *The Scarlet Letter* in September of 1849. His original plan, apparently, was to have it be about two hundred pages in length and to publish it simply as one of the tales in *Old-Time Legends*. But James T. Fields of the firm of Ticknor and Fields, after seeing the partly completed manuscript in November or December of that same year, persuaded Hawthorne to elaborate on the story and publish it as a separate work. Encouraged by Fields's enthusiasm, Hawthorne worked so unremittingly that on January 15, 1850, he was able to write Fields that he was sending "the manuscript portion of my volume"—minus the last three chapters. Fields immediately set his compositors to work. The book, in other words, was being put into type before the last three chapters were written. Undismayed, Hawthorne kept at the task and finished the last chapter on February 3. In view of the careful organization of the narrative and the density of its style, the speed of composition is altogether remarkable. It was a work of almost total commitment. Later Hawthorne was to remember that writing the last part had moved him so profoundly that when he read the conclusion to Sophia his voice "swelled and heaved" and Sophia, saddened by the last events, went to bed with a headache.

Apparently "The Custom House" was originally intended to be the introduction for *Old-Time Legends*. As early as June 5, 1849, Hawthorne wrote Longfellow that he meant to revenge himself in print on his political enemies. Whether he began "The Custom House" that soon cannot be determined, but it was probably finished before Hawthorne became immersed in the writing of *The Scarlet Letter*. Certainly it was complete by January 15, 1850. The reasons for its being included in the same volume as *The Scarlet Letter* are not altogether certain, though Hawthorne had made it clear to Fields that he was not sure that *The Scarlet Letter* by itself would make a saleable volume. Quite probably both Hawthorne and Fields recognized that it could serve as an admirable introduction to the longer work since it gives credence to *The Scarlet Letter* by identifying some of the imaginary events of the story with actual events of New England history. What seems apparent, too, is that Hawthorne felt "The Custom House," by providing a lightness of touch, would make the volume more attractive. In this he was quite right. Partly because of its factual content and partly because of its brightly satirical style, many of his contemporaries preferred "The Custom House" to *The Scarlet Letter*.

III   *Form and Content*

Hawthorne called *The Scarlet Letter* a romance, not a novel. The distinction is an important one if we are to understand the kinds of material that he includes. In "The Custom House" he suggests that life seen in the sunlight is the stuff of the novel; the familiar seen in the moonlight and warmed slightly by the light of the coal fire is the stuff of the romance. In the preface to *The House of the Seven Gables* he says the same thing more literally. The novel is aimed at a minute fidelity to the ordinary course of man's experience; the romance permits a modest use of the "marvelous" or imaginary. The imaginary, though, must be the evanescent flavor of the dish and not the dish itself. Furthermore, the romance like the novel must not swerve from the truths of the human heart and must subject itself to artistic laws. With these pronouncements in mind we may expect that *The Scarlet Letter* will be based on actual life, that its delineation of life will be colored somewhat by the intrusion of the "marvelous," that the story will nevertheless reveal inner or psychological truth, and that the narrative will give artistic form to the confusion of actual experience. All of these we do find.

The story is set in New England in the 1640s. Charles Ryskamp's essay on New England sources (pp. 19-34) indicates in detail how fully Hawthorne depended upon actual persons, places, and events. For his own purposes Hawthorne altered here and there, but there is no mistaking the fact that the setting is Boston of the seventeenth century. No other place or time could possibly be substituted. Yet this is not an historical romance in the usual sense, for there are too many touches of the imaginary. The supernatural is suggested by such happenings as the A in the sky and possibly on Dimmesdale's breast, the sunlight that seeks out Pearl but avoids Hester, the final descent of Chillingworth into the realm of his diabolical master. Borrowings from the Gothic novel add weirdness and even horror. The prison, for example, is grim enough to be a medieval keep, and Governor Bellingham's house is decorated with "cabalistic figures and diagrams"; Mistress Hibbins is gifted with occult insight; Chillingworth is deformed; there are portraits that seem more like the ghosts than the pictures of departed worthies; and there is a strong suggestion of intrigue and murder. The last comes from the introduction of persons and events that parallel those connected with the murder of Sir Thomas Overbury in 1613.[1] To keep all these manifestations—and many more—of the "marvelous" from becoming the dish itself, Hawthorne is careful to see that quantitatively the probable far outweighs the improbable. More than that, he invariably introduces the improbable by attributing it to others: "spectators testified" or "it was whispered by those who peered after." Most importantly, he offers the reader a multiple choice, a natural explanation for every supernatural one.

---

[1] For a full account of these parallels, see Alfred S. Reid, *The Yellow Ruff and The Scarlet Letter* (Gainesville: University of Florida Press, 1955).

This rose-bush, by a strange chance, has been kept alive in history; but whether it had merely survived out of the stern old wilderness, so long after the fall of the gigantic pines and oaks that originally overshadowed it,—or whether, as there is fair authority for believing, it had sprung up under the footsteps of the sainted Anne Hutchinson, as she entered the prison door,—we shall not take upon us to determine.

The basic architecture of the book can be explained in a variety of ways, all of them leading inevitably to the conclusion that Hawthorne was a meticulous craftsman. Gordon Roper in the selection included in this volume (pp. 49-52) sees the structure as having four parts (Chapters I-VIII, IX-XII, XIII-XX, XXI-XXIV), with a different agent or character forcing the action in each part. Leland Schubert (pp. 53-54) describes the book as a frame story with the three scaffold scenes giving order to the sections within the frame. Hugh N. Maclean (pp. 54-55) finds that three epic quests give the book its unique form. Malcom Cowley calls the book a drama of dark necessity in five acts, and Rudolphe von Abele argues that the journey motif is basic to the organization of the story.[2]

Reinforcing the organization, however it is defined, is a complexity of literary devices that gives the book its extraordinary unity and movement. Hawthorne, for example, carefully employs panoramic or generalized narration to set up his highly focused scenes. The panoramic narration of Chapter XIII ("Another View of Hester"), to cite one example, adroitly prepares the reader for the scenes along the seashore and in the forest; similarly, the panoramic narration of Chapter XXI ("The New England Holiday") is preparation for the last scaffold scene. The story achieves artistic completeness and a sense of great climax by having the whole town present at the scaffold in the first and last scenes. Between these two scenes movement is gained not only by the action but, more important, by the dramatic changes in the characters as a result of the action: Chillingworth from humanity to diabolism, Hester from resentfulness to acquiescence, Dimmesdale from cowardice to courage, and Pearl from being a symbol to being a member of the human race.

The restricted setting helps to give the book its remarkable unity. The concentration is upon the little village of Boston in the 1640s, and, for the most part, the rest of the world is forgotten. More than that, it is upon the activities, relationships, and inner states of only four residents of that village. Frequent foreshadowings additionally bind the work together, as does the central symbol, the scarlet letter itself. The scarlet letter is almost always present whether it is on Hester's gown

---

[2] Malcolm Cowley, *College English*, XIX (October 1957), 11-16; Rudolphe von Abele, *Accent*, XI (Autumn, 1951), 211-27.

or, as some thought, in the sky and on Dimmesdale's breast. Its change in meaning from Adulteress to Able provides one of the basic movements of the book, and certainly one of the forces for coherence. As one wit has it, Hester's scarlet letter becomes her red badge of courage. Color, light and shadow, by symbolizing the emotional states of the major characters, tie the inner and outer worlds together, as do a whole host of other symbols that are remarkably simple and easy to grasp. Other devices that add richness to the story and help tie its parts together are those discussed on pages 57-70 of this book: allegory, irony, ambiguity, dichotomy, and use of archetype.

Nothing, however, unifies *The Scarlet Letter* so thoroughly as its insistent concern with guilt and the effects of guilt on the human psyche. As he had done with most of his tales, Hawthorne began thinking about the book in terms of a theme, not of a plot or even of characters. It was his custom to jot down in his notebooks ideas that he thought might serve as controlling themes for stories, and in the following days and even years to mull these over until he saw how one or another might be built into a narrative. There are many such germinal ideas in his notebooks for the 1840s that he used for *The Scarlet Letter*, some of which are reprinted on pp. 17-18. The most central deal with sin: the unpardonable sin, hidden sin, physical manifestations of moral or spiritual disease, a physical symbol indicating a past sin, the sense of isolation following sin. As these would indicate, Hawthorne is first of all a moralist and the story an exploration of human morality. But Hawthorne was a good deal more than simply a moralist; at the very least he was also a student of human psychology, a Romantic of sorts, a skeptic, and something of a determinist. The narrative is a remarkable blend of these seemingly disparate interests and outlooks.

That *The Scarlet Letter* concerns itself with problems of human morality is hardly surprising. In those years under the eaves Hawthorne had steeped himself in the works of the early New England divines, not to mention the Bible and *Pilgrim's Progress*. He had found their assertions concerning evil and its consequences congenial to his temperament because, despite his friends among the Transcendentalists, he felt evil a reality that one could not explain away. Well aware of his own family traditions, too, he somehow felt that his ancestors would not approve of his being merely a writer of story books. " 'What kind of a business in life,—' " he imagines them murmuring one to the other about him, " 'what mode of glorifying God, or being serviceable to mankind in his day and generation,—may that be? Why, the degenerate fellow might as well have been a fiddler!' " His reading, his temperament, his family tradition, whatever the reasons, his tales written before 1850 almost all have strongly moral themes and are replete with secondary moral insights. "The wages of sin," is the one overriding consideration in almost all of these tales. It would have been strange, indeed, had *The Scarlet Letter* not explored facets of this same subject.

The book, then, first of all is concerned with "the wages of sin." Unlike modern writers, Hawthorne is not so concerned with what causes sin as with what sin causes. The selections in the section entitled "Interpretations" (pp. 71-114) explore this subject in considerable detail. Here we need only emphasize that Hawthorne's treatment of sin, evil, guilt—call it what you will—is far more sophisticated than the treatments to be found in the works of other American writers of his time. He shows sin as being relative, not absolute. It is a subjective thing. One feels a sense of guilt only with respect to what he believes he has sinned against, whether it be God, natural law, the laws and mores of the community, or one's own moral standards. The sense of guilt inevitably brings with it a sense of isolation from what one believes he has sinned against. Thus Dimmesdale feels isolated from God because of his adultery, but Hester does not because she does not believe that her adulterous act was a sin against God. It is a further sign of Hawthorne's sophistication that he shows the effects of sin to be ambiguous. Evil can produce understanding as well as isolation, compassion as well as suffering. It can bind people together as well as separate them. Because of her sin, Hester becomes a far more sympathetic and useful person in the community than she ever would have been had she remained faithful to her husband.

What makes Hawthorne's consideration of guilt and its effect so appealing to modern readers is its psychological validity. For the consequences of guilt in *The Scarlet Letter* are viewed primarily as psychological in nature. A sense of guilt brings loneliness, and few have been able to show as well as Hawthorne how private and bitter loneliness can be. Long before alienation became the favorite theme of American novelists, Hawthorne had shown in *The Scarlet Letter* how it can scorch the sensibilities and immobilize the will. He shows, too, what can flow from loneliness: defiance and rebellion, or escape into intellectual activity, or exquisite suffering, or a driving desire to effect reunion, or a combination of two or more of these. More than this, he indicates that guilt repressed is far more devastating in its effects than guilt openly acknowledged; hence Dimmesdale's agony is far greater than Hester's. It is caused not simply by his refusal to admit his paternity publicly but by his refusal, as Frederick Crews shows (pp. 93-104), to admit to himself that his own libidinous wishes rather than Satan are responsible for his sin.

Hawthorne may have been more of a Romantic in composing *The Scarlet Letter* than he would have admitted. Clearly his sympathies are with Hester as she rebels against the strictures of Puritan law, and as she suggests to Dimmesdale that they set up a new morality on the frontier. Almost in spite of the author (certainly in spite of some of his explicit comments on her behavior) she embodies "the authentic American dream of a new life in the wilderness of the new world, and of self-reliant action to realize that ideal." [3] But Hawthorne's Romanticism admits of only the individual rebel acting out of inner conviction. He has little sympathy for organized reform. Indeed, he makes it clear that Hester, like Chillingworth, would have committed the unpardonable sin had she become the leader of a feminist movement. It is one of Pearl's most important functions to save her mother from becoming a reformer.

Certainly his Romanticism did not include Transcendentalism. If he was attracted by the Transcendentalists' emphasis on the individual and rejection of social convention, there is nothing in *The Scarlet Letter* to indicate an acceptance of their metaphysic. He is far closer to the Puritan belief in the depravity of man than to the Transcendental belief in man's perfectibility. What he is, really, is a skeptic who tends to doubt what man can accomplish either by his reason or by divine inspiration. Chillingworth's intellect leads him only to hell; Dimmesdale's faith secures him only an uneasy position in heaven. Only the human affections seem to be worthy of man's trust, and even they when unsupported by the mind can render a man or woman helpless to cope with the depravity of others. Like the true skeptic Hawthorne suggests the viability of the middle way, of temperance and moderation. Hester finally prospers because she combines the head and the heart, with the balance tipped on the side of the heart.

Hawthorne's determinism is rigorous enough to suggest that the human will has only limited choices available to it, but not so rigorous as the determinism of later naturalistic novels in which the individual has no choice. With the Calvinists he substantially agreed that man is inherently sinful. Nevertheless, man seems to have a choice with respect to a particular sin. Chillingworth was not forced to marry Hester. But once a sin is committed, a long train of consequences is inevitable. Chillingworth is aware of this fact. "Nay, from the moment when we came down the old church steps together, a married pair," he says to Hester, "I might have beheld the bale-fire of that scarlet letter blazing at the end of our path!" Hester and Dimmesdale are not forced to commit adultery, but once they do so their sin is bound to intensify and to spawn other sins. Does one have enough freedom of choice so that by an act of will he can bring the consequences of a particular sin to an end? The stories of Dimmesdale and Hester suggest that such freedom of choice is granted man. First one must have a sense of respon-

[3] For development of the idea that Hawthorne's moralism clashed with his Romanticism, see Frederick I. Carpenter, "Scarlet A Minus," *American Literature and the Dream* (New York, 1955), pp. 63-72.

sibility for one's transgression strong enough to energize the will; then he must repent and voluntarily perform such penance as seems appropriate. Even this procedure in the Hawthornian world, though, may not wipe the slate altogether clean. At least Dimmesdale believes it vain to hope that he and Hester can meet in heaven in "an everlasting and pure reunion." In this regard, at least, Hawthorne's determinism is darker than that of the early Puritans since they felt confident that through God's grace the elect could be washed of their sins and participate in everlasting joy.

The Scarlet Letter is not a perfect book. Hawthorne himself thought it too gloomy, and many modern readers complain of Pearl's unreality, of the explicit moralizing, and of the catch-all ending so reminiscent of the "round-up" in the last chapter of a sentimental novel. Still, in any listing of the best American novels, using the word loosely, *The Scarlet Letter* invariably appears among the first five.

IV   Reception and Reputation

As one might suspect, the most popular works of the early 1850s were such sentimental and didactic novels as Susan Warner's *The Wide, Wide World* (1850), Mrs. E. D. E. N. Southworth's *The Curse of Clifton* (1852), Harriet Beecher Stowe's *Uncle Tom's Cabin* (1852), Maria S. Cummins' *The Lamplighter* (1854), all of them written by those Hawthorne referred to grumpily as "a damned mob of scribbling women." But *The Scarlet Letter*, if very considerably less popular, was well received. What is more, since it first appeared in 1850 it has never been out of print.

The first edition of 2500 copies appeared in March, and was sold out within three days. Apparently even Ticknor and Fields, the publishers, had not expected this kind of response since nearly three-fourths of the type was distributed and had to be reset for the second edition, which was published April 22. The second edition consisted of 2500 copies also. In September a third edition of 1000 copies was printed from stereotype plates, a sure sign that the publishers finally realized they had a book with a continuing sale. Causes for this substantial beginning are not hard to find. Because he had been unfairly fired from his position at the Boston Custom House Hawthorne was probably the best known writer in the country. He could be sure of a sympathy vote —or sale, in this case. Ticknor and Fields, in addition, had indulged in some rather fancy prepublication advertising beginning as early as December 29, 1849—well over a month before the book was finished. A three-column advertisement appeared in the *New York Literary World* four times in February 1850. Moreover, most of the reviews of *The Scarlet Letter* were favorable. The most influential, possibly, were those by Evert A. Duyckinck in *The Literary World* (March 30, 1850), George Ripley in the New York *Daily Tribune* (April 1, 1850), and Edwin P. Whipple in *Graham's Magazine* (May 1850). Ironically A. C. Coxe may have boosted the sales more than these favorable reviewers by announcing in the *Church Review* (January 1851) that it was "a dirty book." Any work suggesting adultery in its title was more daring in the 1850s than we now can believe possible. Finally, of course, the excellence of the book itself contributed substantially to its sales. Whatever the reasons, *The Scarlet Letter* began relatively well, though it was certainly no best seller. During the remaining thirteen years of Hawthorne's life, American printings totalled only 7,800 copies. At 15 per cent on a retail price of seventy-five cents Hawthorne's entire earnings from it slightly exceeded $1,500.[4] English editions, because there were no international copyright laws, earned him nothing.

Over the years interest in *The Scarlet Letter* has increased rather than waned. Many of the tales and *The House of the Seven Gables* got into the schoolroom sooner because their themes were more genteel, but *The Scarlet Letter* has always been the favorite with the critics. In the nineteenth century its greatest boost came from Henry James, who in his critical biography of Hawthorne declared that the narrative "has the beauty and harmony of all original and complete conceptions, and its weaker spots, whatever they are, are not of its essence; they are mere light flaws and inequalities of surface. One can often return to it; it supports familiarity, and has the inexhaustible charm and mystery of great works of art. It is admirably written."

Readers of the nineteenth century valued the book primarily as a depiction of colonial culture and as a demonstration of the bitter fruits of moral transgression. In both instances they oversimplified. They took the picture of the 1640s too literally, not realizing that Hawthorne was adjusting history to suit what he called his allegory. The unfortunate result of such simplification was that Americans generally came to think of the Puritans as being far gloomier than they really were, far more obsessed with the subjects of depravity and damnation than they really were. Also, few of the earlier critics saw the ambiguity in Hawthorne's depiction of sin. For them the sin of Hester and Dimmesdale was a relatively simple thing bringing inevitable suffering of a predictable nature to the sinners. In their behalf, however, it should be added that many of the early readers and critics viewed

---

[4] All of the figures in this paragraph have been taken from William Charvat's Introduction to the Centenary Edition of *The Scarlet Letter* (Columbus: The Ohio State University Press, 1962).

the book as an outstanding literary achievement. If they found it a bit gloomy, they were nevertheless pleased that here finally was a work by an American author that could stand with the best being produced in England.

In our own time, the popularity of the book continues to grow. In 1966 there were twenty-four editions on the market, the most authoritative being the Centenary Edition published by the Ohio State University Press. Criticism of *The Scarlet Letter* has become much more varied and more sophisticated. Readers have discovered that it yields rich rewards to almost every kind of critical approach. The literary historians have found it useful in studying the Romantic movement and, more particularly, the traditions of the Gothic, the historical, and the sentimental novel. The New Critics have discovered that Hawthorne's flair for neatness of organization gives them material for analysis such as they seldom find outside of the lyric poem. Readers interested in psychology, especially Freudian psychology, turn to it as a fascinating and illuminating study of repression. Readers interested in archetypes can find them here, and those interested in symbols have a field day since there is hardly a concrete detail in the book that fails to have more than one level of meaning. Social critics interested in the work of art as a depiction of a particular culture have discovered that it is a rewarding task to determine how Hawthorne pictured—and distorted—the life of seventeenth century New England. Present-day moralists have found exciting subtleties in Hawthorne's treatment of sin that eluded earlier readers. Only the philosophically minded reader has found the book thin, and for a good reason. Interested primarily in man's moral and psychological dilemmas, Hawthorne left metaphysical considerations for others. Finally, critical approaches aside, today's reader finds Hawthorne's skeptical temperament congenial. In his doubts about the possibilities of the human mind, in his awareness of human loneliness, in his insight into the enormous complexities of the human psyche, in his great regard for human affection, in his assumptions about life that approach those of modern existentialism, in all of these ways and others Hawthorne speaks directly to our own age. *The Scarlet Letter*, therefore, remains a book to be read not as a monument in literary history but as a work unceasingly capable of engaging the mind and the emotions.

This collection cannot by any means include all of the works which have commented fruitfully upon the form or the content of *The Scarlet Letter*. Confronted with strict limitations on space I have simply tried to assemble representative selections under the rubrics of Background, Form, Techniques, and Interpretations. Limited in number as they are, my hope is that these selections nevertheless will help readers to explore *The Scarlet Letter* more perceptively and, consequently, more enjoyably.

My thanks are due to the authors and publishers of the works included here. They responded to my requests with such uniform courtesy and helpfulness that the task of obtaining permissions became not a chore but a heartwarming correspondence with friends. I am grateful, too, to Professor Maynard Mack, who suggested this volume to me, and who made valuable suggestions for its contents. Particularly I should like to thank Mrs. Dorotha Dilkes, my research assistant. I could not have undertaken the book had she not been willing to assume responsibility for the details of its creation.

J. C. G.

University of Iowa
Iowa City, Iowa

PART ONE

Background

FIRST APPEARANCE OF THEMES
IN *The Scarlet Letter*

Nathaniel Hawthorne:
From *The American Notebooks*

To symbolize moral or spiritual disease by disease of the body;—thus, when a person committed any sin, it might cause a sore to appear on the body;—this to be wrought out.

[October 27, 1841]

Pearl—the English of Margaret—a pretty name for a girl in a story.

[1842?]

In moods of heavy despondency, one feels as if it would be delightful to sink down in some quiet spot, and lie there forever, letting the soil gradually accumulate and form a little hillock over us, and the grass and perhaps flowers gather over it. At such times, death is too much of an event to be wished for;—we have not spirits to encounter it; but choose to pass out of existence in this sluggish way.

[1842?]

The Unpardonable Sin might consist in a want of love and reverence for the Human Soul; in consequence of which, the investigator pried into its dark depths, not with a hope or purpose of making it better, but from a cold philosophical curiosity,—content that it should be wicked in whatever kind or degree, and only desiring to study it out. Would not this, in other words, be the separation of the intellect from the heart?

[1844]

The life of a woman, who, by the old colony law, was condemned always to wear the letter A, sewed on her garment, in token of her having committed adultery.

[1845?]

A story of the effects of revenge, in diabolizing him who indulges in it.

[November 17, 1847]

First Appearance of Hester in Hawthorne's Works

Nathaniel Hawthorne:
From "Endicott and the Red Cross"

In close vicinity to the sacred edifice appeared that important engine of Puritanic authority, the whipping-post—with the soil around it well trodden by the feet of evil doers, who had there been disciplined. At one corner of the meeting-house was the pillory, and at the other the stocks; and, by a singular good fortune for our sketch, the head of an Episcopalian and suspected Catholic was grotesquely incased in the former machine; while a fellow-criminal, who had boisterously quaffed a health to the king, was confined by the legs in the latter. Side by side, on the meeting-house steps, stood a male and a female figure. The man was a tall, lean, haggard personification of fanaticism, bearing on his breast this label,—A WANTON GOSPELLER,—which betokened that he had dared to give interpretations of Holy Writ unsanctioned by the infallible judgment of the civil and religious rulers. His aspect showed no lack of zeal to maintain his heterodoxies, even at the stake. The woman wore a cleft stick on her tongue, in appropriate retribution for having wagged that unruly member against the elders of the church; and her countenance and gestures gave much cause to apprehend that, the moment the stick should be removed, a repetition of the offence would demand new ingenuity in chastising it.

The above-mentioned individuals had been sentenced to undergo their various modes of ignominy, for the space of one hour at noonday. But among the crowd were several whose punishment would be life-long; some, whose ears had been cropped, like those of puppy dogs; others, whose cheeks had been branded with the initials of their misdemeanors; one, with his nostrils slit and seared; and another, with a halter about his neck, which he was forbidden ever to take off, or to conceal beneath his garments. Methinks he must have been grievously tempted to affix the other end of the rope to some convenient beam or bough. There was likewise a young woman, with no mean share of beauty, whose doom it was to wear the letter A on the breast of her gown, in the eyes of all the world and her own children. And even her own children knew what that initial signified. Sporting with her in-

famy, the lost and desperate creature had embroidered the fatal token
in scarlet cloth, with golden thread and the nicest art of needlework;
so that the capital A might have been thought to mean Admirable, or
anything rather than Adulteress.

The Nature of the Romance

Nathaniel Hawthorne: From the Preface to *The House of the Seven Gables*

When a writer calls his work a Romance, it need hardly be observed
that he wishes to claim a certain latitude, both as to its fashion and
material, which he would not have felt himself entitled to assume had
he professed to be writing a Novel. The latter form of composition is
presumed to aim at a very minute fidelity, not merely to the possible,
but to the probable and ordinary course of man's experience. The
former—while, as a work of art, it must rigidly subject itself to laws,
and while it sins unpardonably so far as it may swerve aside from the
truth of the human heart—has fairly a right to present that truth
under circumstances, to a great extent, of the writer's own choosing or
creation. If he think fit, also, he may so manage his atmospherical
medium as to bring out or mellow the lights and deepen and enrich
the shadows of the picture. He will be wise, no doubt, to make a very
moderate use of the privileges here stated, and, especially, to mingle
the Marvellous rather as a slight, delicate, and evanescent flavor, than
as any portion of the actual substance of the dish offered to the public.
He can hardly be said, however, to commit a literary crime even if he
disregard this caution.

Sources for Details

Charles Ryskamp: The New England Sources of *The Scarlet Letter*

After all the careful studies of the origins of Hawthorne's tales and

"The New England Sources of The Scarlet Letter," *by Charles Ryskamp.* Ameri-
can Literature, *XXXI (November 1959), 257-72. Copyright © 1959 by the Duke
University Press. Reprinted by permission of the Duke University Press and Charles
Ryskamp.*

the extensive inquiry into the English sources of *The Scarlet Letter*,[1] it is surprising that the American sources for the factual background of his most famous novel have been largely unnoticed. As would seem only natural, Hawthorne used the most creditable history of Boston available to him at that time, and one which is still an important source for the identification of houses of the early settlers and for landmarks in the city. The book is Dr. Caleb H. Snow's *History of Boston*. Study and comparison of the many histories read by Hawthorne reveal his repeated use of it for authentication of the setting of *The Scarlet Letter*. Consequently, for the most part this article will be concerned with Snow's book.

If we are to see the accurate background Hawthorne created, some works other than Snow's must also be mentioned, and the structure of time as well as place must be established. Then it will become apparent that although Hawthorne usually demanded authentic details of colonial history, some small changes were necessary in his portrayal of New England in the 1640s. These were not made because of lack of knowledge of the facts, nor merely by whim, but according to definite purposes—so that the plot would develop smoothly to produce the grand and simple balance of the book as we know it.

During the "solitary years," 1825-37, Hawthorne was "deeply engaged in reading everything he could lay his hands on. It was said in those days that he had read every book in the Athenaeum. . . ." [2] Yet no scholar has studied his notebooks without expressing surprise at the exceptionally few remarks there on his reading. Infrequently one will find a bit of "curious information, sometimes with, more often without, a notation of the source; and some of these passages find their way into his creative work." [3] But for the most part Hawthorne did not reveal clues concerning the books he read and used in his own stories. About half of his writings deal in some way with colonial American history, and Professor Turner believes that "Haw-

---

[1] I shall make no reference to the English sources of *The Scarlet Letter* which have been investigated by Alfred S. Reid in *The Yellow Ruff and The Scarlet Letter* (Gainesville, 1955) and in his edition of *Sir Thomas Overbury's Vision . . . and Other English Sources of Nathaniel Hawthorne's "The Scarlet Letter"* (Gainesville, 1957). Most of this article was written before the publication of Reid's books. It may serve, however, as a complement or corrective to the central thesis put forth by Reid: "that accounts of the murder of Sir Thomas Overbury were Hawthorne's principal sources in composing *The Scarlet Letter*" (*The Yellow Ruff*, p. 112). The page references in my text to *The Scarlet Letter* are to the Riverside edition (Boston, 1883).

[2] James T. Fields, *Yesterdays with Authors* (Boston, 1900), p. 47. For a list of books which Hawthorne borrowed from the Salem Athenaeum, see Marion L. Kesselring, *Hawthorne's Reading 1828-1850* (New York, 1949). All of my sources are included in this list, except the second edition (1845) of Felt's *Annals of Salem*.

[3] *The American Notebooks*, ed. Randall Stewart (New Haven, 1932), p. xxxii.

thorne's indebtedness to the history of New England was a good deal larger than has ordinarily been supposed." [4] Certainly in *The Scarlet Letter* the indebtedness was much more direct than has hitherto been known.

Any work on the exact sources would have been almost impossible if it had not been for Hawthorne's particular use of the New England annals. Most of these are similar in content. The later historian builds on those preceding, who, in turn, must inevitably base all history on the chronicles, diaries, and records of the first settlers. Occasionally an annalist turns up a hitherto unpublished fact, a new relationship, a fresh description. It is these that Hawthorne seizes upon for his stories, for they would, of course, strike the mind of one who had read almost all the histories, and who was intimate with the fundamentals of colonial New England government.

As a young bachelor in Salem Hawthorne, according to his future sister-in-law, Elizabeth Peabody, "made himself thoroughly acquainted with the ancient history of Salem, and especially with the witchcraft era." [5] This meant that he studied Increase Mather's *Illustrious Providences* and Cotton Mather's *Magnalia Christi Americana.* He read the local histories of all the important New England towns. He read —and mentioned in his works—Bancroft's *History of the United States,* Hutchinson's *History of Massachusetts,* Snow's *History of Boston,* Felt's *Annals of Salem,* and Winthrop's *Journal.*[6] His son reported that Hawthorne pored over the daily records of the past: newspapers, magazines, chronicles, English state trials, "all manner of lists of things. . . . The forgotten volumes of the New England Annalists were favorites of his, and he drew not a little material from them." [7] He used these works to establish verisimilitude and greater materiality for his own books. His reading was perhaps most often chosen to help him—as he wrote to Longfellow—"give a life-like semblance to such shadowy stuff" [8] as formed his romances. Basically it was an old method of achieving reality, most successfully accomplished in his own

[4] H. Arlin Turner, "Hawthorne's Literary Borrowings," *PMLA,* LI (June 1936), 545.

[5] Moncure D. Conway, *Life of Nathaniel Hawthorne* (New York, 1890), p. 31.

[6] Edward Dawson, *Hawthorne's Knowledge and Use of New England History: A Study of Sources* (Nashville, Tenn., 1939), pp. 5-6; Turner, p. 551.

[7] Julian Hawthorne, *Hawthorne Reading* (Cleveland, 1902), pp. 107-8, 111, 132. Hawthorne's sister Elizabeth wrote to James T. Fields: "There was [at the Athenaeum] also much that related to the early History of New England. . . . I think if you looked over a file of old Colonial Newspapers you would not be surprised at the fascination my brother found in them. There were a few volumes in the Salem Athenaeum; he always complained because there were no more" (Randall Stewart, "Recollections of Hawthorne by His Sister Elizabeth," *American Literature,* XVI [January 1945], 324, 330).

[8] *The American Notebooks,* p. xlii.

day by Scott; but for Hawthorne the ultimate effects were quite different. Here and there Hawthorne reported actual places, incidents, and people—historical facts—and these were united with the creations of his mind. His explicitly stated aim in *The Scarlet Letter* was that "the Actual and the Imaginary may meet, and each imbue itself with the nature of the other" (p. 55). His audience should recognize "the authenticity of the outline" (p. 52) of the novel, and this would help them to accept the actuality of the passion and guilt which it contained. For the author himself, the strongest reality of outline or scene was in the past, especially the history of New England.

The time scheme of the plot of *The Scarlet Letter* may be dated definitely. In Chapter XII, "The Minister's Vigil," the event which brings the various characters together is the death of Governor Winthrop. From the records we know that the old magistrate died on March 26, 1649.[9] However, Hawthorne gives the occasion as Saturday, "an obscure night of early May" (pp. 179, 191). Some suggestions may be made as reasons for changing the date. It would be difficult to have a night-long vigil in the cold, blustery month of March without serious plot complications. The rigidly conceived last chapters of the book require a short period of time to be dramatically and psychologically effective. The mounting tension in the mind and heart of the Reverend Mr. Dimmesdale cries for release, for revelation of his secret sin. Hawthorne realized that for a powerful climax, not more than a week, or two weeks at the most, should elapse between the night of Winthrop's death, when Dimmesdale stood on the scaffold, and the public announcement of his sin to the crowd on Election Day. The Election Day (p. 275) and the Election Sermons (p. 257) were well-known and traditionally established in the early colony in the months of May or June.[10] (The election of 1649, at which John Endicott be-

---

[9] William Allen, *An American Biographical and Historical Dictionary* (Cambridge, Mass., 1809), p. 616; Caleb H. Snow, *A History of Boston* (Boston, 1825), p. 104; Thomas Hutchinson, *The History of Massachusetts* (Salem, 1795), I, 142.

[10] John Winthrop, *The History of New England from 1630 to 1649* (Boston, 1825-1826), II, 31, 218 (a note on p. 31 states that the charter of 1629 provided for a general election on "the last Wednesday in Easter term yearly"; after 1691, on the last Wednesday of May); also Daniel Neal, *The History of New-England . . . to . . . 1700* (London, 1747), II, 252. Speaking of New England festivals, Neal writes: "their Grand Festivals are the Day of the annual Election of Magistrats at *Boston,* which is the latter End of *May;* and the Commencement at *Cambridge,* which is the last *Wednesday* in *July,* when Business is pretty much laid aside, and the People are as chearful among their Friends and Neighbours, as the *English* are at *Christmas.*" Note Hawthorne's description of Election Day *(The Scarlet Letter,* p. 275): "Had they followed their hereditary taste, the New England settlers would have illustrated all events of public importance by bonfires, banquets, pageantries and processions. . . . There was some shadow of an attempt of this kind in the mode of celebrating the day on which the political year of the colony commenced.

came governor, was held on May 2.) Consequently Hawthorne was forced to choose between two historical events, more than a month apart. He wisely selected May, rather than March, 1649, for the time of the action of the last half of the book (Chapters XII-XXIII). The minister's expiatory watch on the scaffold is just seven years after Hester Prynne first faced the hostile Puritans on the same platform (pp. 179, 194, 205). Therefore, the first four chapters of *The Scarlet Letter* may be placed in June 1642 (see p. 68). Hawthorne says that at this time Bellingham was governor (pp. 85-86). Again one does not find perfect historical accuracy; if it were so, then Winthrop would have been governor, for Bellingham had finished his term of office just one month before.[11] A possible reason for Hawthorne's choice of Bellingham will be discussed later.

The next major scene—that in which Hester Prynne goes to the mansion of Bellingham—takes place three years later (1645).[12] Hawthorne correctly observes: "though the chances of a popular election had caused this former ruler to descend a step or two from the highest rank, he still held an honorable and influential place among the colonial magistracy" (p. 125).[13] From the description of the garden of Bellingham's house we know that the time of the year was late summer (pp. 132-33).

With these references to time, as Edward Dawson has suggested,[14] we can divide the major action of the novel as follows:

Act One

i. Chapters I-III. The Market-Place, Boston. A June morning, 1642.
ii. Chapter IV. The Prison, Boston. Afternoon of the same day.

Act Two

Chapters VII-VIII. The home of Richard Bellingham, Boston. Late summer, 1645.

Act Three

i. Chapter XII. The Market-Place. Saturday night, early May 1649.

The dim reflection of a remembered splendor, a colorless and manifold diluted repetition of what they had beheld in proud old London . . . might be traced in the customs which our forefathers instituted, with reference to the annual installation of magistrates."

[11] Winthrop, II, 31: June 2, 1641, Richard Bellingham elected governor. Winthrop, II, 63: May 18, 1642, John Winthrop elected governor.

[12] *The Scarlet Letter*, p. 138: "Pearl, therefore, so large were the attainments of her three years' lifetime, could have borne a fair examination in the New England Primer, or the first column of the Westminster Catechisms, although unacquainted with the outward form of either of those celebrated works." The Westminster Catechisms were not formulated until 1647; the New England Primer was first brought out ca. 1690.

[13] Winthrop, II, 220: on May 14, 1645, Thomas Dudley had been elected governor.

[14] I am largely indebted to Dawson, p. 17, for this time scheme.

ii. Chapters XIV-XV. The sea coast, "a retired part of the peninsula" (p. 202). Several days later.

iii. Chapters XVI-XIX. The forest. Several days later.

Act Four

Chapters XXI-XXIII. The Market-Place. Three days later (see p. 257).

The place of each action is just as carefully described as is the time. Hawthorne's picture of Boston is done with precise authenticity. A detailed street-by-street and house-by-house description of the city in 1650 is given by Snow in his *History of Boston*. It is certainly the most complete history of the early days in any work available to Hawthorne. Whether he had an early map of Boston cannot be known, but it is doubtful that any existed from the year 1650. However, the

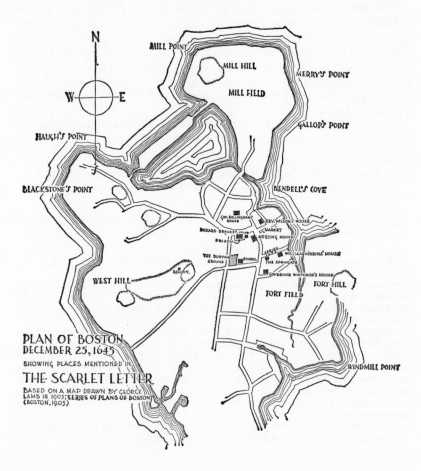

City of Boston Records, 1634-1660, and the "Book of Possessions" with the reconstructed maps (made in 1903-1905 by George Lamb, based on the original records) [15] prove conclusively the exactness of the descriptions written by Snow and Hawthorne.

Hawthorne locates the first scene of *The Scarlet Letter* in this way:

> . . . it may be safely assumed that the forefathers of Boston had built the first prison-house somewhere in the vicinity of Cornhill, almost as seasonably as they marked out the first burial-ground, on Isaac Johnson's lot, and round about his grave, which subsequently became the nucleus of all the congregated sepulchres in the old churchyard of King's Chapel. (p. 67)[16]
>
> It was no great distance, in those days, from the prison-door to the market-place. . . . Hester Prynne . . . came to a sort of scaffold, at the western extremity of the market-place. It stood nearly beneath the eaves of Boston's earliest church, and appeared to be a fixture there. (pp. 75-76)[17]

Snow says that in 1650 Governor Bellingham and the Rev. John Wilson lived on one side of the Market-Place and Church Square (Snow, p. 117). Near Spring Lane on the other side of the Square (mentioned by Hawthorne when little Pearl says, "I saw her, the other day, bespatter the Governor himself with water, at the cattle-trough in Spring Lane," p. 164) was the home of Governor Winthrop (Snow, p. 108). All the action of *The Scarlet Letter* set in Boston is thus centered in the heart of the city. This, as Snow takes great pains to point out, was where all the leading townsmen lived. He writes:

> It has been so often repeated that it is now generally believed the north part of the town was at that period the most populous. We are convinced that the idea is erroneous. . . . The book of possessions records the estates of about 250, the number of their houses, barns, gardens, and sometimes the measurement of their lands. It seems to embrace the pe-

[15] For the drawing of the map reproduced with this article, I am grateful to Professor W. F. Shellman, Jr., of the School of Architecture, Princeton University.

[16] Concerning Isaac Johnson, Snow writes: "According to his particular desire expressed on his death bed, he was buried at the Southwest corner of the lot, and the people exhibited their attachment to him, by ordering their bodies to be buried near him. This was the origin of the first burying place, at present the Chapel burial ground" (p. 37).

[17] Justin Winsor, in *The Memorial History of Boston* (Boston, 1881), I, 506, 539, writes: "The whipping-post appears as a land-mark in the Boston records in 1639, and the frequent sentences to be whipped must have made the post entirely familiar to the town. It stood in front of the First Church, and was probably thought to be as necessary to good discipline as a police-station now is. . . . The stocks stood sometimes near the whipping-post. . . . And here, at last, before the very door of the sanctuary, perhaps to show that the Church and State went hand-in-hand in precept and penalty, stood the first whipping-post,—no unimportant adjunct of Puritan life."

riod from 1640 to 1650, and we conclude, gives us the names of almost, if not quite, all the freemen of Boston. They were settled through the whole length of the main street on both sides. . . . It is evident too, that most of the wealthy and influential characters lived in what is now the centre of the town. We discover only about thirty names of residents north of the creek. (pp. 128-29)

A clear instance of Hawthorne's borrowing a fact from Snow is in the naming of "Master Brackett, the jailer" (p. 92). Few colonial historians mention a jailer in Boston at this time, and if they do, they give his name as Parker. But Snow, alone it would seem, gives this information about Brackett, after writing about the property of John Leverett: "His next neighbour on the south was Richard Parker or Brackett, whose name we find on the colony records as prison keeper so early as 1638. He had 'the market stead' on the east, the prison yard west, and the meeting house on the south" (Snow, p. 116). This last sentence taken from Snow gives the exact location of the action of the early chapters of *The Scarlet Letter*.

Another example of Hawthorne's use of Snow is shown in the description of Governor Bellingham's house. Here Hawthorne builds a vivid image of the old mansion. He writes of Hester and Pearl:

> Without further adventure, they reached the dwelling of Governor Bell-ingham. This was a large wooden house, built in a fashion of which there are specimens still extant in the streets of our older towns. . . . It had, indeed, a very cheery aspect; the walls being overspread with a kind of stucco, in which fragments of broken glass were plentifully inter-mixed; so that, when the sunshine fell aslant-wise over the front of the edifice, it glittered and sparkled as if diamonds had been flung against it by the double handful. . . . It was further decorated with strange and seemingly cabalistic figures and diagrams, suitable to the quaint taste of the age, which had been drawn in the stucco when newly laid on, and had now grown hard and durable, for the admiration of after times. (pp. 128-29)[18]

There are almost no representations of the first settlers' houses in the New England annals. But Snow on one occasion does print an old plate showing an "Ancient building at the corner of Ann-Street and Market-Square" (p. 166). And he describes the house in a way which bears a remarkable resemblance to the sketch written by Hawthorne twenty-five years later:

> This, says a description furnished by a friend, is perhaps the only wooden building now standing in the city to show what was considered elegance of architecture here, a century and a half ago. . . . The outside is cov-

[18] Hawthorne also accurately noted that Governor Bellingham was "bred a lawyer" (p. 131). Snow writes of Bellingham: "He was by education a lawyer" (p. 159).

ered with plastering, or what is commonly called rough-cast. But instead of pebbles, which are generally used at the present day to make a hard surface on the mortar, broken glass was used. This glass appears like that of common junk bottles, broken into pieces of about half an inch diameter. . . . This surface was also variegated with ornamental squares, diamonds and flowers-de-luce. (p. 167)[19]

Snow is also the only historian who tells the story of Mrs. Sherman's pig in order to bring out its effect upon the early Massachusetts government.[20] Hawthorne, with his characteristic interest in the unusual fact from the past, refers to this strange incident:

> At that epoch of pristine simplicity, however, matters of even slighter public interest, and of far less intrinsic weight, than the welfare of Hester and her child, were strangely mixed up with the deliberations of legislators and acts of state. The period was hardly, if at all, earlier than that of our story, when a dispute concerning the right of property in a pig not only caused a fierce and bitter contest in the legislative body of the colony, but resulted in an important modification of the framework itself of the legislature. (p. 126)

In his version of the story Snow said that the incident "gave rise to a change also in regard to the Assistants" (p. 95) and that because of the confusion and dissatisfaction over the decision of the court, "provision was made for some cases in which, if the two houses differed, it was agreed that the major vote of the whole should be decisive. This was the origin of our present Senate" (p. 96).

The characters named in *The Scarlet Letter*—other than Hester, Pearl, Chillingworth, and Dimmesdale, for whom we can find no real historical bases—were actual figures in history. The fictional protagonists of the action move and gain their being in part through their realistic meetings with well-known people of colonial Boston. Even the fantastic Pearl grows somewhat more substantial in the light of the legend and story of her primitive world. She is seen, for example, against the silhouette of the earlier Mr. Blackstone. When describing Bellingham's garden Hawthorne relates: "There were a few rose-bushes, however, and a number of apple-trees, probably the descendants of those planted by the Reverend Mr. Blackstone, the first settler of the peninsula; that half-mythological personage, who rides through our early annals, seated on the back of a bull" (p. 133). Snow had said:

---

[19] For a possible source for details concerning the interior of Bellingham's house, the front door, knocker, etc., see Joseph B. Felt, *Annals of Salem*, 2nd ed. (Salem, 1845), I, 403-6.

[20] Snow, pp. 95-96. Hutchinson, I, 135-36 also refers to the incident, but not in this particular way.

By right of previous possession, Mr. Blackstone had a title to proprietor-
ship in the whole peninsula. It was in fact for a time called Blackstone's
neck. . . . Mr. Blackstone was a very eccentrick character. He was a man
of learning, and had received episcopal ordination in England. . . . It
was not very long before Mr. Blackstone found that there might be more
than one kind of nonconformity, and was virtually obliged to leave the
remainder of his estate here. . . . Let the cause of his removal have
been what it may, certain it is that he went and settled by the Pawtucket
river. . . . At this his new plantation he lived uninterrupted for many
years, and there raised an orchard, the first that ever bore apples in Rhode
Island. He had the first of the sort called yellow sweetings, that were ever
in the world, and is said to have planted the first orchard in Massachusetts also. . . . Though he was far from agreeing in opinion with Roger
Williams, he used frequently to go to Providence to preach the gospels;
and to encourage his younger hearers, while he gratified his own benevolent disposition, he would give them of his apples, which were the first
they ever saw. It was said that when he grew old and unable to travel on
foot, not having any horse, he used to ride on a bull, which he had
tamed and tutored to that use. (pp. 50-53)

This account is taken virtually word for word from a series of articles
called "The Historical Account of the Planting and Growth of Providence" published in the Providence *Gazette* (January 12 to March 30,
1765).[21] However, Snow adds to this narrative the application to
Boston, which would be of special interest to Hawthorne (the phrase,
"and is said to have planted the first orchard in Massachusetts also").
    The only minor characters that are developed to such an extent
that they become in any way memorable figures are Mrs. Hibbins
and the Rev. John Wilson. Hawthorne's use of Mrs. Hibbins shows
again a precise interest in the byways of Boston history. He describes
the costume of the "reputed witch-lady" carefully (pp. 264, 286). He
refers to her as "Governor Bellingham's bitter-tempered sister, . . .
the same who, a few years later, was executed as a witch" (p. 144).
And again, during the minister's vigil, Hawthorne writes that
Dimmesdale beheld "at one of the chamber-windows of Governor
Bellingham's mansion . . . the appearance of the old magistrate himself. . . . At another window of the same house, moreover, appeared
old Mistress Hibbins, the Governor's sister . . ." (p. 181). In Snow's
book there is this account of Mrs. Ann Hibbins:

The most remarkable occurrence in the colony in the year 1655 was the
trial and condemnation of Mrs. Ann Hibbins of Boston for witchcraft.
Her husband, who died July 23, 1654, was an agent for the colony in
England, several years one of the assistants, and a merchant of note in
the town; but losses in the latter part of his life had reduced his estate,

[21] These were reprinted in the Massachusetts Historical Society's *Collections*, 2nd
Ser., IX (1820), 166-203.

and increased the natural crabbedness of his wife's temper, which made her turbulent and quarrelsome, and brought her under church censures, and at length rendered her so odious to her neighbours as to cause some of them to accuse her of witchcraft. The jury brought her in guilty, but the magistrates refused to accept the verdict; so the cause came to the general court, where the popular clamour prevailed against her, and the miserable old lady was condemned and executed in June 1656. (p. 140).[22]

There seems to be only one source for Hawthorne's reference to Mrs. Hibbins as Bellingham's sister. That is in a footnote by James Savage in the 1825 edition of John Winthrop's *History of New England,* and it was this edition that Hawthorne borrowed from the Salem Athenaeum.[23] Savage writes that Mrs. Hibbins "suffered the punishment of death, for the ridiculous crime, the year after her husband's decease; her brother, Bellingham, not exerting, perhaps, his highest influence for her preservation." [24] Hawthorne leads the reader to assume that Mrs. Hibbins, nine years before the death of her husband, is living at the home of her brother. Hawthorne uses this relationship between Bellingham and Mrs. Hibbins in order to have fewer stage directions and explanations. It helps him to establish a more realistic unity in the tale. It partially explains the presence of the various people at the Market-Place the night of the minister's vigil, since Bellingham's house was just north of the scaffold. It also suggests why Bellingham is the governor chosen for the opening scenes of the novel, to prevent the plot from becoming encumbered with too many minor figures.

The Reverend John Wilson's description is sympathetically done, and it is for the most part historically accurate. Hawthorne presents him as "the reverend and famous John Wilson, the eldest clergyman of Boston, a great scholar, like most of his contemporaries in the profession, and withal a man of kind and genial spirit" (p. 86). Cotton Mather,[25] William Hubbard,[26] and Caleb Snow testify to his remarkable "compassion for the distressed and . . . affection for all" (Snow, p. 156). William Allen, in his *American Biographical and Historical Dictionary,* writes that "Mr. Wilson was one of the most hum-

[22] This is almost a literal copy from Hutchinson, I, 173. See also William Hubbard, "A General History of New England," Massachusetts Historical Society *Collections,* 2nd Ser., V (1815), 574; Winthrop, I, 321.

[23] Kesselring, p. 64.

[24] Winthrop, I, 321n. This contradicts Julian Hawthorne's observation: "As for Mistress Hibbins, history describes her as Bellingham's relative, but does not say that she was his sister, as is stated in the 'Romance'" ("Scenes of Hawthorne's Romances," *Century Magazine,* XXVIII [July 1884], 391).

[25] *Magnalia Christi Americana* (London, 1702), bk. III, p. 46.

[26] Hubbard, p. 604.

ble, pious, and benevolent men of the age, in which he lived. Kind
affections and zeal were the prominent traits in his character. . . .
Every one loved him. . . ." [27] Hawthorne, to gain dramatic opposition to Dimmesdale, makes the preacher seem older than he really
was. He pictures the man of fifty-seven as "the venerable pastor, John
Wilson . . . [with a] beard, white as a snow-drift" (p. 134); and later,
as the "good old minister" (p. 182).

Hawthorne's description of Puritan costuming has been substan-
tiated by twentieth century research. Although the elders of the colonial church dressed in "sad-colored garments, and gray, steeple-
crowned hats" (p. 67)[28] and preached simplicity of dress, Hawthorne
recognized that "the church attendants never followed that preaching." [29] "Lists of Apparell" left by the old colonists in their wills, in-
ventories of estates, ships' bills of lading, laws telling what must *not*
be worn, minister's sermons denouncing excessive ornamentation in
dress, and portraits of the leaders prove that "little of the extreme
Puritan is found in the dress of the first Boston colonists." [30] Alice
Morse Earle, after going over the lists of clothing brought by the Puritans, concludes:

> From all this cheerful and ample dress, this might well be a Cavalier
> emigration; in truth, the apparel supplied as an outfit to the Virginia
> planters (who are generally supposed to be far more given over to rich
> dress) is not as full nor as costly as this apparel of Massachusetts Bay. In
> this as in every comparison I make, I find little to indicate any difference
> between Puritan and Cavalier in quantity of garments, in quality, or
> cost—or, indeed, in form. The differences in England were much exag-
> gerated in print; in America they often existed wholly in men's notions
> of what a Puritan must be. (I, 34)

Hawthorne's descriptions agree with the early annals. The embroideries and bright colors worn by Pearl, the silks and velvets of Mrs. Hibbins, Hester's needlework—the laces, "deep ruffs . . . and gorgeously
embroidered gloves"—were, as he said, "readily allowed to individ-

---

[27] Allen, p. 613. The Reverend John Wilson was born in 1588; he died in 1667.

[28] The phrase, "steeple-crowned hats," is used by Hawthorne each time he describes the dress of the Puritan elders (*The Scarlet Letter*, pp. 24, 67, 79, 278). The
only source that I have been able to find for this particular phrase is in an essay
on hats in a series of articles on clothing worn in former times: Joseph Moser,
"Vestiges, Collected and Recollected, Number XXIV," *European Magazine*, XLV
(1804), 409-15. The Charge-Books of the Salem Athenaeum show that Hawthorne
read the magazine in which this article appeared. Moser wrote about the "elevated
and solemn beavers of the Puritans" (p. 414) and the "high and steeple-crowned
hats, probably from an idea, that the conjunction of Church and State was necessary to exalt their archetype in the manner that it was exalted" (p. 411).

[29] Alice Morse Earle, *Two Centuries of Costume in America* (New York, 1903), I, 8.

[30] Earle, I, 13.

uals dignified by rank or wealth, even while sumptuary laws forbade
these and similar extravagances to the plebeian order" (pp. 105-6).
The Court in 1651 had recorded "its utter detestation and dislike that
men or women of mean condition should take upon them the garb
of Gentlemen, by wearing gold or silver lace . . . which, though al-
lowable to persons of greater Estates or more liberal Education, yet
we cannot but judge it intolerable in persons of such like condition." [31] Hawthorne's attempt to create an authentic picture of the
seventeenth century is shown in *The American Notebooks* where he
describes the "Dress of an old woman, 1656." [32] But all of Hawthorne's
description is significant beyond the demands of verisimilitude. In
The Scarlet Letter he is repeating the impressions which are characteristic of his tales: the portrayal of color contrasts for symbolic purposes, the play of light and dark, the rich color of red against black,
the brilliant embroideries[33] on the sable background of the "sad-
colored garments."

So far there has been slight mention of the influence of Cotton
Mather's writings on *The Scarlet Letter*. These surely require our attention in any study such as this one. Professor Turner believes that
certain elements of Mather's *Magnalia Christi Americana*, "and in
particular the accounts of God's judgment on adulterers [in II, 397-
98], may also have influenced *The Scarlet Letter*. Mather relates [II,
404-5] that a woman who had killed her illegitimate child was ex-
horted by John Wilson and John Cotton to repent while she was in
prison awaiting execution. In like manner, as will be recalled, John
Wilson joins with Governor Bellingham and Arthur Dimmesdale in
admonishing Hester Prynne to reveal the father of her child." [34] It is
possible that an echo of the witch tradition in the *Magnalia Christi
Americana* may also be found in *The Scarlet Letter*. "The proposal
by Mistress Hibbins that Hester accompany her to a witch meeting is
typical of the Mather witch tradition, which included, in accordance
with the well known passage in *The Scarlet Letter*, the signing in the
devil's book with an iron pen and with blood for ink. . . ." [35] The

[31] Winsor, I, 484-85. Hawthorne had read the *Acts and Laws . . . of the Massa-
chusetts-Bay in New-England* (Boston, 1726)—see Kesselring, p. 56.
[32] *The American Notebooks*, p. 109.
[33] One of Hawthorne's favorite words—for example, see *The American Notebooks*, p. 97.
[34] Turner, p. 550; Turner is using the Hartford (1855) edition of the *Magnalia
Christi Americana*. See *The Scarlet Letter*, pp. 86-91.
[35] Turner, p. 546—see *The Scarlet Letter*, pp. 143-44, and *Magnalia Christi Americana*, bk. VI, p. 81: "It was not long before *M. L.* . . . confess'd that *She* rode with
her Mother to the said Witch-meeting. . . . At another time *M. L. junior*, the
Grand-daughter, aged about 17 Years . . . declares that . . . they . . . rode on a
Stick or Pole in the *Air* . . . and that they set their Hands to the Devil's Book. . . ."

Black Man mentioned so often by Hawthorne (pp. 100, 144, 222-25) was familiar to the Puritan settlers of New England. Pearl tells her mother "a story about the Black Man. . . . How he haunts this forest, and carries a book with him,—a big, heavy book, with iron clasps; and how this ugly Black Man offers his book and an iron pen to everybody that meets him here among the trees; and they are to write their names with their own blood" (p. 222). Concerning the Black Man, Cotton Mather had written: "These *Tormentors* tendred unto the afflicted a *Book*, requiring them to *Sign* it, or *Touch* it at least, in token of their consenting to be Listed in the Service of the *Devil;* which they refusing to do, the *Spectres* under the Command of that *Blackman,* as they called him, would apply themselves to Torture them with prodigious Molestations." [36]

Even the portent in the sky, the great red letter A, which was seen on the night of the revered John Winthrop's death (and Dimmesdale's vigil), would not have seemed too strange to Puritan historians. To them it would certainly not have been merely an indication of Hawthorne's gothic interests. Snow had related that when John Cotton had died on Thursday, December 23, 1652, "strange and alarming signs appeared in the heavens, while his body lay, according to the custom of the times, till the Tuesday following" (p. 133).

The idea of the scarlet A had been in Hawthorne's mind for some years before he wrote the novel. In 1844 he had made this comment in his notebooks as a suggestion for a story: "The life of a woman, who, by the old colony law, was condemned always to wear the letter A, sewed on her garment, in token of her having committed adultery." [37] Before that, in "Endicott and the Red Cross," he had told of a "woman with no mean share of beauty" who wore a scarlet A. It has commonly been accepted that the "old colony law" which he had referred to in his notebooks had been found in Felt's *Annals of Salem,* where we read under the date of May 5, 1694: "Among such laws, passed this session, were two against Adultery and Polygamy. Those guilty of the first crime, were to sit an hour on the gallows, with ropes about their necks,—be severely whipt not above 40 stripes; and forever after wear a capital A, two inches long, cut out of cloth coloured differently from their clothes, and sewed on the arms, or back parts of their garments so as always to be seen when they were about." [38]

Exactly when Hawthorne began writing *The Scarlet Letter* is not

---

[36] *Magnalia Christi Americana*, bk. II, p. 60; see also Massachusetts Historical Society *Collections*, V (1708), 64; Neal, II, 131, 133-35, 144, 150, 158, 160, 169.

[37] *The American Notebooks*, p. 107.

[38] Joseph B. Felt, *The Annals of Salem, from Its First Settlement* (Salem, 1827), p. 317.

known, but by September 27, 1849, he was working on it throughout
every day. It was finished by February 3, 1850.[39] In the novel there is
the same rapid skill at composition which is typical of the notebooks.
From the multitude of historical facts he knew he could call forth
with severe economy only a few to support the scenes of passion or
punishment. Perhaps it does not seem good judgment to claim that
Hawthorne wrote *The Scarlet Letter* with a copy of Snow's *History of
Boston* on the desk. But it does not appear believable that all these
incidental facts from New England histories, the exacting time scheme,
the authentic description of Boston in the 1640s, should have remained so extremely clear and perfect in his mind when he was under
the extraordinary strain of writing the story. Here the studies of
Hawthorne's literary borrowings made by Dawson, Turner, and others
must be taken into account. They have shown that in certain of his
tales, he "seems to have written with his original open before him." [40]
To claim a firm dependence upon certain New England histories for
the background of *The Scarlet Letter* should therefore not seem un-
reasonable.

The incidents, places, and persons noticed in this article are the
principal New England historical references in *The Scarlet Letter*. A
study like this of Hawthorne's sources shows something of his thor-
ough method of reading; it reveals especially his certain knowledge of
colonial history and his interest in the unusual, obscure fact. But
these are sidelights of an author's mind. His steady determination was
to make the romances of his imagination as real as the prison-house
and the grave.

It would be unfair to leave the study of Hawthorne's historical approach here. His final concern in history was the attempt to find the
"spiritual significance" [41] of the facts. As his sister Elizabeth had said
of the young man: "He was not very fond of history in general." [42]
Hawthorne stated concretely his conception of history and the novel
in a review (1846) of W. G. Simms's *Views and Reviews in American
History*:

> . . . we cannot help feeling that the real treasures of his subject have
> escaped the author's notice. The themes suggested by him, viewed as he
> views them, would produce nothing but historical novels, cast in the same
> worn out mould that has been in use these thirty years, and which it is
> time to break up and fling away. To be the prophet of Art requires
> almost as high a gift as to be a fulfiller of the prophecy. Mr. Simms has

---

[39] Randall Stewart, *Nathaniel Hawthorne* (New Haven, 1948), pp. 93-95.
[40] Turner, p. 547.
[41] Julian Hawthorne, *Hawthorne Reading*, p. 100.
[42] "Recollections of Hawthorne by His Sister Elizabeth," p. 324.

not this gift; he possesses nothing of the magic touch that should cause new intellectual and moral shapes to spring up in the reader's mind, peopling with varied life what had hitherto been a barren waste.[43]

With the evocation of the spirit of the colonial past, and with a realistic embodiment of scene, Hawthorne repeopled a landscape wherein new intellectual and moral shapes could dwell. The new fiction of Hester Prynne and the old appearances of Mrs. Hibbins could not be separated. Time past and time present became explicable as they were identified in the same profound moral engagement.

[43] Stewart, "Hawthorne's Contributions to *The Salem Advertiser*," *American Literature*, V (January 1934), 331-32.

PURITANISM

Joseph Schwartz:
Three Aspects of Hawthorne's Puritanism

That Nathaniel Hawthorne had been charged with being a Puritan either emotionally, imaginatively, or dogmatically is a commonplace in Hawthorne scholarship. It began when James Russell Lowell called him a "Puritan Tieck," and when Herman Melville, his sometime friend, seeing more deeply into his own personality than into Hawthorne's, found his appeal in "blackness, ten times more black . . . that Calvinistic sense of Innate Depravity and Original Sin, from whose visitations, in some shape or other, no deeply thinking mind is always and wholly free." But this judgment was repudiated even then by the members of Hawthorne's family and by his intimate friends. Sophia, his wife, Julian, his son, James T. Fields, his publisher, and Horatio Bridge, his closest friend, did much to dispel the cloud of gloom that the label "Puritan" was soon to affix to his works. Henry Bright, a British friend, called him "the *least* morbid of men," and his judgment was echoed by Elizabeth Peabody, Hawthorne's sister-in-law. In the first major critical study made of Hawthorne's work (1879), Henry James made a special effort to distinguish between Hawthorne's pronounced consciousness of sin and Puritanism. The notebooks, James contended, testify to his "serenity and amenity of

"Three Aspects of Hawthorne's Puritanism," by *Joseph Schwartz.* New England Quarterly, *XXXVI (June 1963), 192-208. Copyright © 1963 by the* New England Quarterly. *Reprinted by permission of the* New England Quarterly *and Joseph Schwartz.*

mind." James was specifically answering M. Emile Montégut who, writing in the *Revue des Deux Mondes,* had called Hawthorne "Un Romancier Pessimiste." James felt that there was nothing to show that Hawthorne held bitter or morbid views. "The development of Hawthorne's mind was not toward sadness." The results of pessimism —"the note of depression, of despair, of the disposition to undervalue the human race"—cannot be found in the character of Hawthorne's mind and imagination.[1] Despite the fact that James's *Hawthorne* is regarded by many as one of the best critical studies ever made of an American writer, the issue of Hawthorne's Puritanism was not completely settled to the satisfaction of post-Jamesian scholars.

The great interest in Hawthorne in the twentieth century led to frequent and distinguished reappraisals of his work, including, of course, new evaluations of his Puritanism. "Puritanism" had become by now a convenient tag to apply to any writer who has either a deep consciousness of sin or a belief in original sin, which in turn has become confused with a belief in innate depravity, a position which varies greatly from the general tradition of Christian belief. It is largely because of this false identification and because of a misreading of Hawthorne's own challenge to unqualified optimism, that such a twentieth century critic as Harry Levin sees, as Melville did, the overwhelming power of blackness in Hawthorne. Alexander Cowie agrees in part: "A modified predestination he also found a convenient basis for explaining man's apparent inability to cope successfully with regeneration in this world." Certainly such a strange phrase as "modified predestination" would seem to need some explanation. It is, on the face of things, a philosophic impossibility. In another study, Austin Warren tells us that Hawthorne appears to have been "in imaginative sympathy" with the "great Calvinistic doctrine of predestination." Mark Van Doren tends to agree with Mr. Warren. Yet, Carl Van Doren would have us reject this idea: "He had little Puritanism left in him. Dealing with many of its problems, he reached his own verdicts. His humane moralism looked at old prejudices with new eyes." Randall Stewart feels that he accepted some form of belief in depravity and predestination. Arlin Turner would agree with this. But Yvor Winters says simply that Hawthorne turned "his back upon the excessively simplified conceptions of his Puritan ancestors." So the critical war goes on.[2]

[1] Henry James, *Hawthorne* (Ithaca, N.Y., 1956), 21-22.
[2] These opinions are found in Harry Levin, *The Power of Blackness* (New York, 1958), pp. 10, 26; Alexander Cowie, *The Rise of the American Novel* (New York, 1948), p. 356; Austin Warren, *Nathaniel Hawthorne* (New York, 1934), p. xxi; Mark Van Doren, *The Best of Hawthorne* (New York, 1941), p. 11; Carl Van Doren, *What is American Literature?* in *The Viking Portable Van Doren* (New York,

There are understandable reasons for this disagreement over such an important idea. In stories that appear side by side, Hawthorne apparently seems to condemn and admire Puritanism. But if we are to believe that he is not completely contradictory, there must be a reason for his peculiar ambivalence. Some order can be made out of what is only an apparent contradiction, if we remember that Hawthorne's differing attitudes toward Puritanism refer specifically to different facets of this one large concept. Puritanism was not a theology alone. Although it became the American branch of Calvinism, it also gave its name to a characteristic way of life. And, for Hawthorne, Puritanism was also associated with the American struggle for political liberty. Thus, his comments on Puritanism cannot be adequately treated unless we understand that his discussion is manifestly limited to three specific areas: (1) Puritanism as a theology of predestination and universal depravity; (2) Puritanism as a way of life; (3) Puritanism as it was involved in the early struggle for political liberty in America.

Hawthorne's nonfictional attitude toward Puritanism in general can be indicated simply, if not thoroughly, because there are only a few instances of his discussion of it. He tells us of a conversation he had with G. P. R. James, the novelist, concerning the Puritans, "about whom we agreed pretty well in our opinions."[3] James later wrote him a note asking him to come to a haymaking, admonishing him to leave his "grim old Puritans" at home. In another instance, he recorded that it was difficult to write a lively and entertaining book for children when he had such unmalleable material as the somber, stern, and rigid Puritans with which to work.[4] It is not too fruitful, however, to pursue a study of his generalizations. It is better to look at the various facets of Puritanism which we can discover from a close reading of his works.

It is not a simple matter to piece together Hawthorne's attitude toward Puritanism as a theology of predestination and personal depravity. He was no formal critic of religion nor a practiced theologian. Despite some very direct statements, it is chiefly by implication that we can discover his critical position concerning these matters. His

---

1945), p. 590; Randall Stewart, *Nathaniel Hawthorne: A Biography* (New Haven, 1948), pp. 244ff.; Arlin Turner, "Hawthorne and Reform," *New England Quarterly*, XV (1942), 708; and Yvor Winters, *In Defense of Reason* (New York, 1947), p. 174.

[3] *The American Notebooks by Nathaniel Hawthorne*, edited by Randall Stewart (New Haven, 1932), pp. 232-33.

[4] *The Complete Writings of Nathaniel Hawthorne*, The Old Manse Edition, ed. H. E. Scudder (Boston, 1900) XII, XXIV. Subsequent references to Hawthorne's writings will be to this edition and will be indicated by volume and page numbers inserted parenthetically in the text.

attitude toward the Puritan religion is further complicated by his universally recognized rejection of Unitarianism, the "new" religion, opposed to the "old" orthodoxy, as seen in one of his best satires, "The Celestial Railroad." Because the cold scorn with which he treats Unitarianism in this story is unmistakable, some of his commentators have been led to assert that he chose the old while opposing the new. That he rejected both has not often been recognized as a possibility, despite that fact that he called Calvinism a "lump of lead" and Unitarianism "a feather" in the same passage. Neither "variety of the black-coated tribe" captured his allegiance (IV, 24-26). It still remains a crucial matter to demonstrate that he found neither solace nor comfort in the religion of his ancestors.

Hawthorne always felt that the religious system of Puritanism was hard, cold, and confined; it was only the fervent faith of firm believers that redeemed it all. He seems to praise the attitude of the individual believer, but not the system of belief. We see this illustrated in "Main Street" in his analysis of the Puritan meetinghouse. "A meaner temple," he writes, "was never consecrated to the worship of the Deity." As long as their individual faith was strong, "as long as their lamps were kindled at the heavenly flame," they were able to give a radiance to the place. But even in the time of the first generation, and certainly in their children's time, "these lamps began to burn more dimly." Then it could be seen clearly "how hard, cold, and confined was their system,—how like an iron cage was that which they called Liberty" (III, 75-76). The obvious use of symbol here points up Hawthorne's disapproval of the idea which the material object represents. That he approved of sincere faith or belief is apparent, but his approval of this specific form of religion is another matter. He did make some comments about the principal theological tenets of the Puritan which can help us to discover his attitude.

Hawthorne knew enough of their theology to have Governor Bellingham mention depravity as an essential tenet of the Puritan religion in *The Scarlet Letter*. When the eminent townsmen are deciding whether or not to take Pearl away from Hester, Bellingham is abashed by Pearl's liberal and elfin responses to his attempt to discover how well she knows the accepted religion. "This is awful!" he cries, because a child of three cannot tell him who made her. "Without question, she is equally in the dark as to her soul, its present depravity, and future destiny!" (VI, 159-60) It cannot be merely an artistic accident that in this scene, when the pompous Bellingham parades the universal depravity of the soul before her, Hester Prynne is given a chance to contradict him. She seems not to be depraved, but has a clear choice between good and evil: follow Mistress Hibbins into the

forest and meet "the Black Man," or choose a life of service for the
good of Pearl. She chooses the good, even though she indicates that
she might have freely gone to the Devil if she had lost Pearl.

It is in this same novel that Hawthorne gives evidence of his knowledge of another important tenet of Puritan theology. Chillingworth,
"a fiend," becomes the spokesman for the Puritan doctrine of necessity
which flows from the concept of predestination. He tries to silence
Hester's arguments for allowing the Minister a second chance. It is not
granted to me to pardon, he tells her. "My old faith, long forgotten,
comes back to me, and explains all that we do and suffer." Since the
first step awry, "it has all been a dark necessity" (VI, 250). It cannot
be argued that Hawthorne approves of this doctrine because of Chillingworth's statement of it. In fact, the contrary seems to be true. Chillingworth is the villain of the piece, a man who has turned himself
into a fiend, a man whom the others in the novel see as evil. He uses
the apology of his old faith to escape personal responsibility for his
sin, a sin which at another time he freely admits as his own.

The positive side of predestination—arbitrary and exclusive election—was just as inimical to Hawthorne's delicate sense of men's
equality. In a character study, "The Man of Adamant," that ranks in
power with "Ethan Brand," he satirizes intolerance and the exclusiveness of those who feel that they alone are the elect. This attitude,
which made the "saved one" shrink from the contamination of mankind, was directly opposed to Hawthorne's sense of universal brotherhood. Richard Digby, the man of adamant, thought that he had the
only key to salvation; that, indeed, it was folly for men to trust to
their own strength or to any other belief. Digby was a member of that
stern brotherhood (mentioned in "Main Street") that fled England
for America; but he was the most intolerant of his fellows. Imagining
that he was the only one who could be saved, he soon fled to the forest
where he lived alone. His theology, granted the orientation of Puritanism, was carefully logical though not very humane. He rejects
friendship, kindness, and love because of his insane self-righteousness
and the certainty of his predestined election. Hawthorne compares
his notion of salvation, appropriately, to a plank in a tempestuous sea
which Digby bestrode triumphantly, hurling anathemas against the
rest of the wretches of mankind who were struggling in the sea of
death. The plank is so narrow that he takes special care to keep it out
of the reach of others. So pleased that Providence had entrusted him
alone with this treasure, "Richard Digby determined to seclude himself to the sole and constant enjoyment of his happy fortune." He
finally turns into a man of stone, a symbol "repelling the whole race
of mortals,—not from heaven,—but from the horrible loneliness of his
dark, cold sepulchre" (III, 226 and 238). The whole legend can be

taken as a satire on any mortal or group of mortals who would exclude the rest of the human race in much the same way that predestination arbitrarily elected those to be saved and damned the rest. This is a manifestation in religion of the sin which Hawthorne hated most, the sin of pride. Richard Digby was proud of his election, of his possession of an exclusive religious idea; Lady Eleanor's mantle is a symbol of social pride or social exclusiveness; and Ethan Brand becomes a symbol of intellectual pride. Any manifestation of this kind of pride is inevitably destructive.

Certain aspects of Richard Digby's state of mind are often referred to as a "holier than thou" attitude. Hawthorne makes special reference to this state of mind in "The Gentle Boy." The author's concern is not with one person as a symbol (as in the case of Digby) but with the whole community of Puritans and the atmosphere which they generate. When the Pearsons adopt Ilbrahim, the gentle Quaker boy, because he is alone in the world, their Christian motivation makes no impression on the rest of the community. The overtones of the New Testament in conflict with the Old in the story cannot be missed. The people avoid contact with little Ilbrahim because they fear contamination. As the chosen, the elect, they do not understand the gospel of love. The mild-featured maidens as well as the stern old men draw away from him lest the sanctuary be polluted by his presence. He is a symbol of "a sweet infant of the skies" who strayed from home, but "all the inhabitants of this miserable world closed their impure hearts against him, drew back their earth-soiled garments from his touch, and said, 'we are holier than thou'" (I, 100). The whole tale is an indictment of harsh, stern, and self-righteous Puritanism, but this one aspect of Puritan exclusiveness is singled out for special attack. In one of the most moving scenes in his short fiction, Hawthorne uses the Puritan children as operative symbols of the sharp cruelty which results from bigoted and fanatic exclusiveness. Ilbrahim made friends with another boy, whose fall from a tree had confined him for his period of recovery to the Pearsons' home. When partially recovered, the invalid completes his convalescence at his own home. Ilbrahim has no other friends and cannot resist trying to join a group of Puritan children at their play. Their mirth stops the moment they see him try to join them, and they rush upon him displaying "an instinct of destruction far more loathsome than the bloodthirstiness of manhood." His former friend, the invalid, stands apart from the group and calls to him, "Fear not, Ilbrahim, come hither and take my hand." With unsullied trust, Ilbrahim strives to obey him. "After watching the victim's struggling approach with a calm smile and unabashed eye, the foul-hearted little villain lifted his staff and struck Ilbrahim on the mouth, so forcibly that the blood issued in a stream."

His arms had been raised to protect himself, but now he dropped
them at once. The injury to his body was severe, but the injury done
to his spirit was worse (I, 119-20).

The community is not content to torment the boy; its members also
interpret the ways of Providence for Tobias Pearson. From their position of rigid righteousness, the New England Pharisees point out that
his domestic sorrows are signs of God's ill-favor. This was a part of the
uncompromising logic of their system. New England offered opportuni-
ties for a man without fortune, and Pearson had found it difficult to
provide for his wife and family in England. This supposed impurity
of motive was responsible for his lack of prosperity here and for the
loss of his children. "Those expounders of the ways of Providence"
attributed his domestic sorrows to his sin. And they were much less
charitable after he adopted a child of "the accursed sect" (I, 96).

Ilbrahim must die, of course, so that his gentle spirit can win in
death what he could not attain in life. Eventually, the once bitter
persecutors can follow the body of Ilbrahim's real mother, whom Hawthorne also has condemned for her "unbridled fanaticism," to her
grave with some real sorrow.

Hawthorne's attitude toward the religious tenets of Puritanism or
Calvinism seemed to color his use of the words themselves. Evidence
shows that he associated things he disliked with the connotations suggested by Calvinism or Puritanism. When he wanted to describe a
cordial clergyman, Rev. Dr. Burroughs, he wrote, "The Doctor is a
most genial old clergyman . . . with nothing Calvinistic about him." [5]
And when he wanted an adjective to portray an unpleasant and outrageously religious woman, "Calvinistic" came to mind; "I led in Mrs.
Bramley-Moore . . . and found her a stupid woman, of vulgar tone,
and outrageously religious—even to the giving away of little tracts,
and lending religious books . . . I could see little to distinguish her
from a rigidly orthodox and Calvinistic woman of New England." [6]
In *Our Old Home* "an exceedingly grim waiter" must be a "genuine
descendant of the old Puritans" and "quite as sour" (XI, 225). The
unpleasant Swiss caretaker of Chillon Castle is "grim and Calvinistic-
looking" (XXII, 383). A Protestant cathedral in Switzerland disturbed
him because of its "Puritanic neatness" which effaced the "majesty
and mystery that belong to an old church" (XXII, 393-94). He feels
that the comparative freedom of the Catholic cathedral is more agree-
able than "the grim formalities of . . . our own meeting-houses"
(XXII, 272). In "Dr. Bullivant" Hawthorne specifically identifies Calvinism with American Puritanism when he refers to the American

---

[5] *American Notebooks*, p. 16.
[6] *The English Notebooks by Nathaniel Hawthorne*, ed. Randall Stewart (New
York, 1941), p. 55.

minister as "a sour old Genevan divine" (XVII, 269). This is accompanied by a bitter commentary on the Puritan sermon, that important means for giving form to Puritan theology.

Hawthorne uses this same technique of association in his fiction as a stylistic device for establishing the reader's mood for accepting the tone of a character portrayal. This is adroitly accomplished in *The House of the Seven Gables* where in every instance that Judge Pyncheon is most hateful, he is compared directly, in looks and actions, with his Puritan ancestors. When the unsavory Colonel Pyncheon dies early in the romance, Hawthorne tells us that "the iron-hearted Puritan, the relentless persecutor, the grasping and strong-willed man, was dead!" (VII, 17 and 338) The portrait of the Colonel, which serves such an important artistic role in the structure of the romance, is described in terms of the sharpest irony. He holds a Bible with one hand and with the other uplifts an iron sword-hilt. "The latter object, being far more successfully depicted by the artist, stood out in far greater prominence than the sacred volume" (VII, 44).

In the light of the foregoing passages, it is not at all difficult to accept Julian Hawthorne's statement that his father found "small succulence" in the "old literary lumber . . . of the old Puritan divines." [7]

The tendency that Hawthorne had for calling unpleasant things "Puritanic" is an indication that he also rejected Puritanism as a way of life, the second area of my inquiry. His habitual reference to the Puritans as "stern-visaged men" and "unkindly-visaged women" sets the tone for his criticism of their way of life. His covering of the whole range of Puritan life is very complete—all the way from the minister to the children of the Puritan community. The evidence is not from one work or confined to one instance; throughout the whole of his fictional and nonfictional work this critical tendency is apparent. The leading member of the Puritan community was the minister, an apt starting point for tracing Hawthorne's comments. They are hardly pleasant ones. In "Young Goodman Brown" the Devil bears "no slight similitude, both in garb and manner, to some grave divine of the New England churches" (IV, 119). In the nonfictional essay, "The Old Manse," his study is described as black, "made still blacker by the grim prints of ministers that hung around" (IV, 4). In "Dr. Bullivant" the minister "goes by like a dark cloud intercepting the sunshine" (XVII, 272). Parson Thumpcushion in "Passages from a Relinquished Work" is bitterly opposed to the world of the imagination represented by the budding author. Hawthorne's criticism of historical personages is just as unpleasant, as seen in his vicious portrait of Cotton

[7] Julian Hawthorne, *Hawthorne Reading* (Cleveland, 1902), p. 25.

Mather in "Alice Doane's Appeal." Mather, astride his horse and following the procession, seems to summarize the spirit which put the
"witches" to their death. He was "so darkly conspicuous, so sternly
triumphant" that he was mistaken for "the visible presence of the
fiend himself." It is not the Devil, Hawthorne tells his listeners, just
his very good friend, Cotton Mather. He represents "all the hateful
features of his time; the one blood-thirsty man, in whom were con-
centrated those vices of spirit and errors of opinion that sufficed to
madden the whole surrounding multitude" (XVI, 242). In another
instance, Hawthorne calls Mather a hard-hearted, pedantic bigot who
exults in the destruction of a group of Catholic Indians, a group
whose worship Hawthorne finds "touching" (XVII, 235).

When Hawthorne singles out one of the ministers for praise, he
selects one who does not possess the rigid, intolerant, and fanatical
Puritanism of the others. The will of God and the welfare of man
can be accomplished with kindliness instead of severity. Thus, Roger
Williams' face "indicates . . . a gentler spirit, kinder and more ex-
pansive" than that of Hugh Peters, a typical Puritan type (III, 80).
Piety need not be gloomy or severe. But it was from the minister, since
he stood at the pinnacle of society, that the community took its tone.
Rev. Mr. Hooper in "The Minister's Black Veil" so impressed the
legislature with his morbidity that "the legislative measures of that
year were characterized by all the gloom and piety of our ancestral
sway" (I, 58).

This was, in essence, Hawthorne's chief complaint against Puritanism as a way of life: it was gloomy, joyless, and rigid. This atmosphere of joyless deportment fixed itself upon the national character in such a way that even people of his own day "have yet to learn
the forgotten art of gayety." The generation next to the early immi-
grants wore the blackest shade of Puritanism and "so darkened the
national visage with it that all the subsequent years have not sufficed
to clear it up" (VI, 337). He notes with his special kind of irony
that on Election Day, a holiday, there was joy among the people sufficient at least to make them appear "scarcely more grave than most
other communities at a period of general affliction" (VI, 333). That
he never forgot the sour and unsympathetic temper of Puritan life is
evident from one of his last works, *Dr. Grimshawe's Secret.* The two
children playing in the graveyard refuse to be intimidated by the
frowning effigies of eminent Puritans. The children are more encouraged by the good-natured smiles of the stone cherubs than "fright-
ened or disturbed by the sour Puritans" (XV, 2-3). Feeling this way, it
is evident why Hawthorne refers to that New England as a "dismal
abode."

In the Puritan way of life, religion and law were almost identical.

The law itself was severe, and severely was it carried out. With mock ignorance Hawthorne remarks that the scene which awaited the adulterous Hester Prynne in *The Scarlet Letter* on her emergence from the prison could betoken nothing short of the execution of a great criminal. But, he adds, "in that early severity of the Puritan character, an inference of this kind could not so indubitably be drawn" (VI, 68). As a result, the mildest and severest acts of public discipline were alike made venerable and awful. He never questions the need for civil law, but he does criticize the Puritan method of enforcing it. The whipping-post and the cat-o'-nine tails, the man condemned to wear visibly a halter around his neck throughout his lifetime, the matronly woman chained to a post to stand all day in the hot sun, the person in the great wooden cage put on display like a wild beast in a zoo— these, he remarks with heavy irony, are "the profitable sights that serve the good people to while away the earlier part of lecture-day" (III, 87-88). In "Endicott and the Red Cross" the whipping-post, significantly, stands next to the meetinghouse. On either side of it are the pillory and the stocks. The usual offenders are present: the wanton gospeller with his label, the woman who wears a cleft stick on her tongue for criticizing the elders, those whose ears have been cropped, whose cheeks have been branded with the initials of their sins, the man with his nostrils seared and slit, and the young woman with the letter "A" on her breast.

But if these scenes are too somber, let us turn to a happier one. Here is Hawthorne's picture in "Main Street" of an "outbreak of grisly jollity" that modified the morbid life of the Puritan community. His irony is obvious and bitter:

> . . . look back through all the social customs of New England, in the first century of her existence, and read all her traits of character; and if you find one occasion, other than a funeral feast, where jollity was sanctioned by universal practice, I shall set fire to my puppet show without another word. . . . Many a cask of ale and cider is on tap, and many a draught of spiced wine and aqua-vitae has been quaffed. Else why should the bearers stagger . . . and the aged pall-bearers, too, as they strive to walk solemnly beside it [the coffin]?—and wherefore do the mourners tread on one another's heels?—and why, if we may ask without offence, should the nose of the Rev. Mr. Noyes, through which he had been delivering the funeral discourse, glow like a ruddy coal of fire? (III, 105-6)

Hawthorne's many casual references to Puritanism bear out this bitter tone in "Main Street," his extended satire on the Puritan way of life. Even his natural affection for children did not prevent him from referring to the little Puritans in *The Scarlet Letter* as "the most intolerant brood that ever lived" (VI, 133). In "The Gentle

Boy" he calls them "a brood of baby-fiends" (I, 119). When Pearl observes them at their play, the children are "disporting themselves in such grim fashion as the Puritan nature would permit"; playing at going to church, scourging the Quakers, taking Indian scalps, "or scaring one another with freaks of imitative witchcraft" (VI, 132).

From this picture of the Puritan way of life, Hawthorne concludes that despite the severe means used to control man's behavior in the Puritan community, "there is no evidence that the moral standard was higher then than now; or, indeed, that morality was so well defined as it has since become." As often as we consider the past, he tells us, "we find it a ruder and rougher age than our own, with hardly any perceptible advantages, and much that gave life a gloomier tinge." In a short passage full of dusky connotations, Hawthorne summarizes his attitude toward the entire picture of Puritan life. "In vain we endeavor to throw a sunny and joyous air over our picture of this period; nothing passes before our fancy but a crowd of sad-visaged people, moving duskily through a dull gray atmosphere" (III, 187-88). We should be happy, he continues, that we did not live in those days. The rigidity of Puritanism "could not fail to cause miserable distortions to the moral nature," the distortions described so well in "Young Goodman Brown," "The Gentle Boy," "The Man of Adamant," "Main Street," and *The Scarlet Letter*. This kind of life, he says, was "sinister to the intellect and sinister to the heart" (III, 89-90).

My third area of inquiry, Puritanism as it was involved in America's struggle for political liberty, has been much studied by American historians. Our debt to the Puritans is an obvious one and must be acknowledged. Hawthorne, too, was aware of this obligation; yet his attitude exhibits a curious ambivalence. Because the Puritans often represented for him the symbol of resistance to British tyranny, he expressed his hearty approval of their actions. But when he dealt with the political life of the Puritan community in itself, he was not nearly so kind.

As to the first point, Hawthorne was never shy in expressing his gratitude to the Puritans for their early political struggle for liberty. Even in *The Scarlet Letter*, a romance which admits very little digression, he interfered with the pace of the story to analyze the political character of the early Puritans. If they were not brilliant, he comments, at least they were politically solid. They had respect for the idea of government, being accustomed to the British political hierarchy. The early governors of Massachusetts stood up for the welfare of the state "like a line of cliffs against a tempestuous tide" (VI, 345). This somber strength is especially praiseworthy because it is one of the chief reasons why these early communities survived in such a wilderness. Elsewhere Hawthorne calls this active temperament a "gold thread in the web" of the "stern old stuff of Puritanism" (VII, 109). Four of Hawthorne's short tales illustrate his approval of the Puritans as significant actors in America's early struggle for political freedom: "Howe's Masquerade," "The Gray Champion," "Endicott and the Red Cross," and "Edward Randolph's Portrait."

"Howe's Masquerade" is a flimsy bit of writing that just barely demonstrates Hawthorne's power to evoke an eerie scene. In the middle of a masquerade ball which General Howe is giving for his British soldiers, the early Puritan governors come back in spirit to the Governor's mansion and march down the steps to the uneasy amazement of the dancers. They are an ominous warning of Howe's coming defeat. Hawthorne is lavish in his praise for these early freedom-lovers who had resisted tyranny in their own day.

In "The Gray Champion," a tale of more substance, Hawthorne forgets that the Puritans were predestinarians and attributes to them the power to shape their own destiny. Sir Edmund Andros and his oppressive counsellors are routed by the mysterious appearance of the aged Gray Champion, a regicide, who, with a strength of spirit which belies any kind of political determinism, tells the people of the Glorious Revolution. The Gray Champion "is the type of New England's hereditary spirit," a spirit that comes to our aid whenever tyranny would oppress us (I, 14).

In "Edward Randolph's Portrait," the venerable selectman tells Lieutenant-Governor Hutchinson that if you meddle with the devil, look out for his claws. Do not surrender the honor of New England to the royal troops. "We will submit to whatever lot a wise Providence may send us,—always, after our own best exertions to amend it" (II, 39). In Hawthorne's admiration for this positive action, we see an implied hostility to political necessity.

"Endicott and the Red Cross" is in some ways the oddest example of the four. The hero of the story would seem to be Endicott, a man of whom Hawthorne did not approve because he was a bigot and an exclusive religionist. In "The Gentle Boy" he is bitter in his portrayal of Endicott as a persecutor of the Quakers. He describes him as a man "of narrow mind and imperfect education, and his uncompromising bigotry was made hot and mischievous by violent and hasty passions." Even worse, he uses his influence unjustly to secure the death of the Quakers. "His whole conduct in respect to them was marked by brutal cruelty" (I, 86). Again in "Mrs. Hutchinson" he singles out Endicott for another barb, comparing him with the man of adamant. "Next is Endicott, who would stand with his drawn sword at the gate of heaven, and resist to the death all pilgrims thither, except they travelled his own path" (XVII, 9). Even in the "Red Cross" tale his fanaticism is contrasted with the gentle kindness of Roger Williams, and he is embarrassed in the middle of his speech about liberty by a poor soul in the stocks who did not worship as the Puritans saw fit— "Call you this liberty of conscience?" But when Endicott rips the red cross from the foreign flag, Hawthorne cannot resist praising this *political* act, "one of the boldest exploits which our history records" (II, 287). There can be no doubt that Hawthorne warmly endorsed the tyranny-resisting character of the Puritans, a role in which politically at least they transcended their theory of predestination.

But Hawthorne was quick to perceive that while they demanded liberty of conscience and freedom in law from their British rulers, they were not willing to extend this same freedom to those who dissented from the Puritan pattern of life. This aspect of their political character Hawthorne condemned. They were not kind rulers nor tolerant. He described the thirteen men who made up the venerable ruling body as "grim rulers." Their grimness was implemented by their stern law, a law that had vigor to support its maxims and power to annihilate its offenders, "a giant of stern features" with an "iron arm" (VI, 110-11). In "Old News" Hawthorne can afford to smile at the foolish ordinances, imposed by the "rigid hand of Puritanism" only because he is far enough away from them in time (III, 189-90). Their intolerance as well as the sternness of the law and the uncompromising rigidity of its execution can best be seen in the relations between the Puritans and the Quakers. Both sought to escape the domination of the Established Church; yet, the Puritans would not give aid or even tolerance to their brothers in dissent. Hawthorne disapproved of the fanaticism of both sects, but he could not tolerate the persecution of any body of people by another group. The Quakers have a new idea, something which always brings persecution, he notes. He pictures a Quaker woman in sackcloth and ashes almost on the point of converting the Puritans. "This matter must be looked to," the elders muse, "else we have brought our faith across the seas with us in vain." His picture of their persecution of Cassandra Southwick is moving; but even more moving is the record of Ann Coleman. Naked from the waist up and bound to the tail of a cart, she is dragged through the main street at the pace of a brisk walk, while the constable follows with a whip of knotted cords, a smile upon his lips each time he flourishes his lash in the air (III, 91-94). This incident, like the whole of "The Gentle Boy," is a vigorous indictment of the Puritan attitude toward the freedom of others.

From Hawthorne's point of view the Puritan way of life, their denial of civil liberty for others, and their theology combined to give an unfavorable aspect to the national character. It created a social system, based upon an identification of law and religion, that trammeled itself as it did the people who lived under it. Hawthorne states this succinctly in describing the Rev. Arthur Dimmesdale: "the framework of his order inevitably hemmed him in" (VI, 289). The regulations, the prejudices—the framework which inevitably hems men in was not to Hawthorne's liking. He would seek religious solace, but not in this order whose embrace was deadly. So he turned his back upon the religion of his ancestors. And although he has given us an unparalleled study of the atmosphere of those times, it is a study filled with anxiety and horror. As a result of looking at the three aspects of Hawthorne's Puritanism, I hope that some of the critical difficulty in approaching his fiction has been minimized. If my suggestions about Hawthorne's attitude toward Puritanism are correct, we will have to search elsewhere for his metaphysical roots as well as for the frame of reference which gave him his personal sense of values.

PART TWO

Form

THE FOUR-PART STRUCTURE

Gordon Roper: From the Introduction to
The Scarlet Letter and Selected Prose Works

. . . It was in creating a form to embody his content that Hawthorne achieved an artistic success that makes *The Scarlet Letter* one of the few fine formal works of fiction in the history of the novel in English before the work of Henry James.

The form grew organically out of his intention of presenting a central theme "diversified no otherwise than by turning different sides of the same dark idea to the reader's eye." In constructing three symbolic characters to present the three different sides of the same dark idea [sin and its consequences] he had three forces to impel his narrative; by placing them in such a community as Puritan seventeenth century Boston, he had a fourth propulsive force. The technical problem now would be to build a structure that would clearly and dramatically present the three disparate sides, and yet impress upon the reader a sense of the organic interaction of the three lines of development, and finally a unity of effect for the narrative as a whole.

His solution was to build a structure in four parts. The first part focused on one force activating the other three forces; this line of action is developed to a climax wherein the dominant force loses its power to activate, and wherein incentive is provided for one of the three hitherto dominated forces to become the new activating force. The second part develops the course of this new force acting on the other three, up to a second climax, where the power to activate passes to a third force; the third part follows the same pattern and in its climax releases the fourth and final force which brings the narration to its dramatic close.

To gain dramatic effectiveness, in each part Hawthorne has focused

the narrative on the conflict between the activating force and only
one of the other three forces; the effect of the activating force on the
remaining two dominated forces is woven into the action indirectly.
Thus in part one, Hawthorne reveals the force of the Puritan community operating on Hester, Chillingworth, and Dimmesdale. Economically, however, the action focuses on the conflict between the
community and Hester. The opening chapter states the "dark idea"
of the narrative in symbolic terms; Chapter II particularizes the "dark
idea" in dramatic terms. Hester Prynne has sinned against the community and the community is punishing her by public isolation on
the scaffold, and by isolation without its boundaries. Hester seems to
submit to the action of her community but the rebellious force that
is within her is suggested. In Chapter III, the force that Chillingworth embodies is introduced in muted fashion, followed in even
more muted terms by the introduction of the potentialities of Dimmesdale; both of these allowed themselves to be dominated by their community without apparent opposition. Chapters V and VI define the
consequences of the community's punishment on Hester in long passages of psychological analysis. Here Hester is shown, superficially
conforming to the values imposed by the community, thus performing
a false penance. Chapters VII and VIII bring the potential conflict
between the community and Hester to a peak when the community
summons Hester before them to decide whether they should deprive
the mother of her child. In Chapter VIII the community forces
Dimmesdale to recognize Hester as a parishioner and as her minister
to plead for her and her child; his acquiescence ironically underlines
his failure to come to her aid in his natural role. The community, as
activator of the narrative to this point, has created an apparent
stability that from their viewpoint should be maintained; consequently they cease here to be the activator in the narrative. But by
their action they have made Chillingworth aware that Dimmesdale
is the man he is searching for, and thus they open the way for a new
force to become activator of the narrative.

In Chapter IX Hawthorne opens a second quarter of his structure
in which Chillingworth is the force that acts on the other characters.
Here again, as in the first quarter, Hawthorne focuses attention upon
one force acting principally on only one of the other characters, sub-
ordinating, in this case, Hester and the community. Chapter IX
analyzes the nature of the force Chillingworth personifies. Chapter X
dramatizes Chillingworth acting upon Dimmesdale; Chapter XI analyzes the psychological reaction in Dimmesdale to the pressures Chillingworth applies. Chapter XII dramatizes these effects, reaching a
climax wherein Dimmesdale is driven in order to escape his suffering,

to undertake an empty penance on the scaffold in the deserted square. The minister fails to exert his own yet unregenerated force, and is led away by Chillingworth. But on the scaffold, Hawthorne has arranged an event which releases a force hitherto suppressed. By joining hands with the minister on the scaffold, Hester's full human sympathies are reawakened.

Her force is now asserted in Chapter XIII and is to dominate the narrative through this third quarter of the book. Chapter XIII analyzes this new force in Hester. Chapter XIV dramatizes the ascendancy of her force over Chillingworth's; she frees herself from his force by renouncing the vow of silence she had made to him. She then turns to act on Dimmesdale. Before she acts, Hawthorne presents another analysis of her power, and then in Chapter XVI she and Dimmesdale are brought together in the forest. Hester tries to force a reunion with him on her terms by planning that they flee the community. Dimmesdale begs her to be his strength and to act for them. He leaves the forest in Chapter XX, in a maze caused by Hester's domination. But at the conclusion of this chapter the last structural force asserts itself, and we are prepared to move into the fourth quarter of the narrative. Hester's domination over the minister is submerged as he works in the dark at his Election Sermon; apparently the regenerating hand of God descends upon him as the dawn breaks, and at last he has the strength and will to act in accord with the dictates of his spirit.

In the fourth and last quarter, Dimmesdale is the force whose actions drive the narrative to its dramatic conclusion on the scaffold. At this point the architectural skill of Hawthorne is apparent; while other quarters followed the pattern of first analyzing the force which is to dominate the quarter, here Hawthorne shifts the viewpoint back onto Hester only to show that her power to act has run out. Chapter XXIII brings her force to its lowest ebb in the entire narrative; at the same time she realizes that the force now lies in Dimmesdale. And from this lowest point in Hester, Hawthorne moves us up to the most dramatic expression of force in the narrative, the final scene on the scaffold. Here Dimmesdale's regeneration gives him the strength to reveal his sin publicly. He is reunited with Hester and Pearl; his hypocritical relation with his community is changed into a true relationship, and he dies, to be reunited with his God.

The last chapter concludes the course of Chillingworth's life; disposes of the future of the Pearl who was made human by Dimmesdale's action on the scaffold. Then in conclusion it refocuses on the pair of forces which it had dealt with as the narrative opened, Hester and her community. We are shown how they effected a compromise in her life and in her burial. She dies, still haunted by the problem of the right relationship between the sexes, which she has come to realize is not her lot to solve in her community and in her time.

The course of the narrative through these four parts is further clarified, and the stages contrasted meaningfully by Hawthorne's repetition of the structural pattern of part one in parts two and three, and, with a significant shift, in part four. The pattern basic to all quarters is first a presentation in nondramatic form of an analysis of the force that dominates the quarter; this is followed by a dramatization of the force acting on one of the other characters directly; this action is followed by an analysis of the effect on the dominated character, and the quarter is concluded by a dramatization of the effect on the dominated character in a climactic scene wherein the activator loses his force and a new activator gains strength and power. Parts two and three are constructed on this pattern with little deviation. Part one, since it is the opening of the narrative, deviates by first presenting a highly symbolic arrangement of the general forces in the narrative, then following it by a dramatic scene showing the general forces personified and in action. Part four deviates by first analyzing not the activating force, Dimmesdale, but rather the ebb of force in Hester who had dominated the action of the third quarter, for the technical reason suggested above.

Hawthorne gave further pattern to his form by building with large blocks of psychological analysis, interspersed with blocks of dramatic action. The patterning led him to create a number of chapters—notably Chapters V, VI, IX, XI, and XIII—in which he focused a full chapter of analysis on one of the central characters. The second and third parts of his structure are introduced by devoting a full chapter of analysis to the character who is to be the dominating force in that structural part. This patterning also led him to create two scenes of dramatic concentration in each of the four parts—usually in the second and the last chapters. Further, he limited his dramatic action to only a few settings—the public square, the prison interior, Hester's cottage, the Governor's mansion, Dimmesdale's apartment, the forest. The scaffold in the public square is the scene of three of the eight or nine big dramatic scenes.[1] This repeated use of a symbolic setting underlines the stages in the development of his dark idea; yet as much is revealed by his contrast of these scaffold scenes with those occurring in three significantly different settings—the Governor's mansion, Dimmesdale's apartment, and, especially, the forest.

---

[1] This has led some critics to find a structure organized around these three scaffold scenes, or organized in a series of tableaux.

THE FRAME STRUCTURE

Leland Schubert: From *Hawthorne, the Artist*

The structural plan of *The Scarlet Letter* is one of its most beautiful and artistic qualities. No really great work of art is absolutely geometric in its composition. Even the "Last Supper" of Leonardo—so neat in its mathematics—is not flawless in this respect. The good artist avoids absolute balance, absolute repetition, absolute rhythm. Hawthorne has come as close to the absolute in *The Scarlet Letter* as he safely could. The novel's introduction, "The Custom House," is at once a part of the story and separate from it. It is joined to the story by its reference to the letter and by its title which sounds and looks like the titles of the chapters in the novel. (This is the only instance in which the introduction to a Hawthorne novel has a specific and descriptive title.) "The Custom House" is separate from the story in that it is not a first chapter; it is frankly introductory. The last chapter of the book is called "Conclusion." It has a chapter number, twenty-four, and is thus structurally tied into the story. But it, too, is separate from the main flow. It is a summary which ties the various threads together; and it leaps ahead in time, it explains what becomes of the characters. It is related to "The Custom House" by a reference to the "manuscript of old date," described in the introduction, and by a mention of Mr. Surveyor Pue who figures in "The Custom House." Thus the introduction and the conclusion constitute a kind of frame around the story of Hester Prynne. It is true that this frame is not built in quite the same way as many of Hawthorne's frames are, and that it is not perfectly balanced. But its two sections are as much separated from the main story as they are related to it; and I think we may treat them either as a structural part of the story or as a frame. For the sake of simplifying the analysis of the novel's structure, I have chosen to think of "The Custom House" and "Conclusion" as a frame, apart from the story itself.

When we make this separation, the pattern of the story becomes clear and beautiful. It is built around the scaffold. At the beginning,

From Hawthorne, the Artist *by Leland Schubert. Chapel Hill: The University of North Carolina Press, 1944, pp. 137-38. Copyright 1944 by The University of North Carolina Press. Reprinted by permission of The University of North Carolina Press and Leland Schubert.*

in the middle, and at the end of the story the scaffold is the dominating point. Just as it literally rises above the market-place, so does it structurally rise out of the novel's plan and attribute pattern to it. In Chapter II, after the very short first chapter, Hester is taken up on the scaffold. In Chapter XII, the middle chapter (when we omit the concluding chapter), Dimmesdale mounts the scaffold. In Chapter XXIII, the last (omitting the conclusion), Dimmesdale takes Hester and Pearl up there with him. These three incidents are, in every sense, the high points of the novel. The middle chapter, number XII, tends to divide the story into two parts (or three parts, counting this middle chapter). This division is logical when we realize that up to Chapter XII neither the reader nor Chillingworth is certain that Dimmesdale is the father of little Pearl; after Chapter XII, there can be no doubt.

THREE EPIC QUESTS

Hugh N. Maclean: From "Hawthorne's
Scarlet Letter: 'The Dark Problem of This Life'"

Hawthorne knew very well that he was dealing with a theme "not less but more heroic" than anything which had yet appeared in American fiction. Consciously or not, he clothed his fable in epic machinery. The tale begins *in medias res;* it develops in twenty-four books, of which the first twelve lead outward and "downward"; the concluding twelve home to the heart and to salvation—for Dimmesdale, at least. At the halfway mark Chillingworth seems to be triumphant; Pearl has been described in terms almost exclusively of uncontrolled, chaotic passion. A number of "solutions," political, theological, even necromantic, have been tried (or suggested) and found wanting. Dimmesdale allows himself to be led away by the leech. But in the concluding twelve chapters all is reversed. Chillingworth steadily declines in power. Pearl's character, though rudderless for a time, is now considered in terms of its potential intelligence and active fiber. The one true solution to "the dark problem" resolves the bewildered despair of the protagonists on a supernatural plane, to which they can

"Hawthorne's Scarlet Letter: *'The Dark Problem of This Life'"* by Hugh N. *Maclean.* American Literature, *XXVII (March 1955), 13-14. Copyright © 1955 by the Duke University Press. Reprinted by permission of the Duke University Press and Hugh N. Maclean.*

be raised only by supernatural aid. This is "epic machinery" without a self-starter. Only God can provide the vital spark.

There are three epic "quests" in the novel. Dimmesdale's search for salvation is a conscious, if largely involuntary quest, which is one long *agon*, pierced (in Chapter XII), by the *pathos* or apparent "death" of his soul, but concluded by the final triumph (really God's triumph) of the struggling "hero." Two other quests turn on the outcome of this central struggle. Chillingworth, the agent of evil, undertakes a conscious and voluntary quest, with the soul of Dimmesdale as object; this mission, appropriately, is perverted in pattern, and ends (after an apparent victory in Chapter XII) in the destruction of the physician. Pearl, who represents man's hopeful future as Chillingworth recalls his bitter and diseased past, has her quest too. It is first announced by Hester: "My child must seek a heavenly Father; she shall never know an earthly one" (Chap. III). This quest, which is unconscious and involuntary, appears doomed for a time. As Dimmesdale falls under Chillingworth's spell, Pearl seeks knowledge, not of any "heavenly Father," but of "the Black Man." At length, of course, she finds her "heavenly Father." After the kiss on the scaffold, Pearl, reconciled to the conditions of life, will not "forever do battle with the world, but be a woman in it" (Chap. XXIII).

PART THREE

Techniques

ALLEGORY AND SYMBOLISM

F. O. Matthiessen: From *American Renaissance*

Why Hawthorne came nearest to achieving that wholeness in *The Scarlet Letter* may be accounted for in various ways. The grounds on which, according to Trollope, its superiority was "plain to anyone who had himself been concerned in the writing of novels" were that here Hawthorne had developed his most coherent plot. Its symmetrical design is built around the three scenes on the scaffold of the pillory. There Hester endures her public shaming in the opening chapter. There, midway through the book, the minister, who has been driven almost crazy by his guilt but has lacked the resolution to confess it, ascends one midnight for self-torture, and is joined by Hester, on her way home from watching at a deathbed, and there they are overseen by Chillingworth. There, also, at the end, just after his own knowledge of suffering has endowed his tongue with eloquence in his great election sermon, the exhausted and death-stricken Dimmesdale totters to confess his sin at last to the incredulous and only half-comprehending crowd, and to die in Hester's arms.

Moreover, Hawthorne has also managed here his utmost approach to the inseparability of elements that James insisted on when he said that "character, in any sense in which we can get at it, is action, and action is plot." Of his four romances, this one grows most organically out of the interactions between the characters, depends least on the backdrops of scenery that so often impede the action in *The Marble Faun*. Furthermore, his integrity of effect is due in part to the incisive contrasts among the human types he is presenting. The sin of Hester and the minister, a sin of passion not of principle, is not the worst in the world, as they are aware, even in the depths of their misery. She feels that what they did "had a consecration of its own"; he knows that at least they have never "violated, in cold blood, the sanctity of a human heart." They are distinguished from the wronged husband in accordance with the theological doctrine that excessive love for things

From American Renaissance *by F. O. Matthiessen. Copyright 1941 by Oxford University Press, Inc. Reprinted by permission.*

which should take only a secondary place in the affections, though
leading to the sin of lust, is less grave than love distorted, love turned
from God and from his creatures, into self-consuming envy and venge-
ful pride. The courses that these three run are also in natural accord
with their characters as worked upon by circumstance. The physician's
native power in reading the human soul, when unsupported by any
moral sympathies, leaves him open to degradation, step by step, from
a man into a fiend. Dimmesdale, in his indecisive waverings, filled as
he is with penance but no penitence, remains in touch with reality
only in proportion to his anguish. The slower, richer movement of
Hester is harder to characterize in a sentence. Even Chillingworth,
who had married her as a young girl in the knowledge that she responded with no love for his old and slightly deformed frame, even
he, after all that has happened, can still almost pity her "for the
good that has been wasted" in her nature. Her purgatorial course
through the book is from desperate recklessness to a strong, placid
acceptance of her suffering and retribution.

But beyond any interest in ordering of plot or in lucid discrimina-
tion between characters, Hawthorne's imaginative energy seems to
have been called out to the full here by the continual correspondences
that his theme allowed him to make between external events and
inner significances. Once again his version of this transcendental habit
took it straight back to the seventeenth century, and made it something more complex than the harmony between sunrise and a young
poet's soul. In the realm of natural phenomena, Hawthorne examined
the older world's common belief that great events were foreboded by
supernatural omens, and remarked how "it was, indeed, a majestic
idea, that the destiny of nations should be revealed, in these awful hi-
eroglyphics, on the cope of heaven." But when Dimmesdale, in his
vigil on the scaffold, beholds an immense dull red letter in the zenith,
Hawthorne attributes it solely to his diseased imagination, which sees
in everything his own morbid concerns. Hawthorne remarks that the
strange light was "doubtless caused" by a meteor "burning out to
waste"; and yet he also allows the sexton to ask the minister the next
morning if he had heard of the portent, which had been interpreted
to stand for Angel, since Governor Winthrop had died during the
night.

Out of such variety of symbolical reference Hawthorne developed
one of his most fertile resources, the device of multiple choice, which
James was to carry so much further in his desire to present a sense of
the intricacy of any situation for a perceptive being. One main source
of Hawthorne's method lay in these remarkable providences, which
his imagination felt challenged to search for the amount of emblem-

atic truth that might lie hidden among their superstitions. He spoke at one point in this story of how "individuals of wiser faith" in the colony, while recognizing God's Providence in human affairs, knew that it "promotes its purposes without aiming at the stage-effect of what is called miraculous interposition." But he could not resist experimenting with this dramatic value, and his imagination had become so accustomed to the weirdly lighted world of Cotton Mather that even the fanciful possibilities of the growth of the stigma on Dimmesdale did not strike him as grotesque. But when the minister "unbreasts" his guilt at last, the literal correspondence of that metaphor to a scarlet letter in his flesh, in strict accord with medieval and Spenserian personifications, is apt to strike us as a mechanical delimitation of what would otherwise have freer symbolical range.

For Hawthorne its value consisted in the variety of explanations to which it gave rise. Some affirmed that the minister had begun a course of self-mortification on the very day on which Hester Prynne had first been compelled to wear her ignominious badge, and had thus inflicted this hideous scar. Others held that Roger Chillingworth, "being a potent necromancer, had caused it to appear, through the agency of magic and poisonous drugs." Still others, "those best able to appreciate the minister's peculiar sensibility, and the wonderful operation of his spirit upon the body," whispered that "the awful symbol was the effect of the ever-active tooth of remorse," gnawing from his inmost heart outward. With that Hawthorne leaves his reader to choose among these theories. He does not literally accept his own allegory, and yet he finds it symbolically valid because of its psychological exactitude. His most telling stroke comes when he adds that certain spectators of the whole scene denied that there was any mark whatever on Dimmesdale's breast. These witnesses were among the most respectable in the community, including his fellow ministers who were determined to defend his spotless character. These maintained also that his dying confession was to be taken only in its general significance, that he "had desired, by yielding up his breath in the arms of that fallen woman, to express to the world how utterly nugatory is the choicest of man's own righteousness." But for this interpretation, so revelatory of its influential proponents, Hawthorne leaves not one shred of evidence.

It should not be thought that his deeply ingrained habit of apprehending truth through emblems needed any sign of miraculous intervention to set it into action. Another aspect of the intricate correspondences that absorbed him is provided by Pearl. She is worth dissecting as the purest type of Spenserian characterization, which starts with abstract qualities and hunts for their proper embodiment;

worth murdering, most modern readers of fiction would hold, since the tedious reiteration of what she stands for betrays Hawthorne at his most barren.

When Hester returned to the prison after standing her time on the scaffold, the infant she had clasped so tightly to her breast suddenly writhed in convulsions of pain, "a forcible type, in its little frame, of the moral agony" that its mother had borne throughout the day. As the story advances, Hawthorne sees in this child "the freedom of a broken law." In the perverseness of some of her antics, in the heartless mockery that can shine from her bright black eyes, she sometimes seems to her harassed mother almost a witch-baby. But Hester clings to the hope that her girl has capacity for strong affection, which needs only to be awakened by sympathy; and when there is some talk by the authorities of taking the wilful child's rearing into their own hands, Hester also clings to her possession of it as both her torture and happiness, her blessing and retribution, the one thing that has kept her soul alive in its hours of desperation.

Hawthorne's range of intention in this characterization comes out most fully in the scene where Hester and the minister have met in the woods, and are alone for the first time after so many years. Her resolution to save him from Chillingworth's spying, by flight together back to England, now sweeps his undermined spirit before it. In their moment of reunion, the one moment of released passion in the book, the beauty that has been hidden behind the frozen mask of her isolation reasserts itself. She takes off the formal cap that has confined the dark radiance of her hair and lets it stream down on her shoulders; she impulsively unfastens the badge of her shame and throws it to the ground. At that moment the minister sees Pearl, who has been playing by the brook, returning along the other side of it. Picked out by a beam of sunlight, with some wild flowers in her hair, she reminds Hester of "one of the fairies, whom we left in our dear old England," a sad reflection on the rich folklore that had been banished by the Puritans along with the maypoles. But as the two parents stand watching their child for the first time together, the graver thought comes to them that she is "the living hieroglyphic" of all they have sought to hide, of their inseparably intertwined fate.

As Pearl sees her mother, she stops by a pool, and her reflected image seems to communicate to her something "of its own shadowy and intangible quality." Confronted with this double vision, dissevered from her by the brook, Hester feels, "in some indistinct and tantalizing manner," suddenly estranged from the child, who now fixes her eyes on her mother's breast. She refuses Hester's bidding to come to her. Instead she points her finger, and stamps her foot, and becomes all at once a little demon of extravagant protest, all of whose wild gestures are redoubled at her feet. Hester understands what the matter is, that the child is outraged by the unaccustomed change in her appearance. So she wearily picks up the letter, which had fallen just short of the brook, and hides her luxuriant hair once more beneath her cap. At that Pearl is mollified and bounds across to them. During the weeks leading up to this scene, she had begun to show an increasing curiosity about the letter, and had tormented her mother with questions. Now she asks whether the minister will walk back with them, hand in hand, to the village, and when he declines, she flings away from his kiss, because he is not "bold" and "true." The question is increasingly raised for the reader, just how much of the situation this strange child understands.

Thus, when the stiff layers of allegory have been peeled away, even Hawthorne's conception of Pearl is seen to be based on exact psychological notation. She suggests something of the terrifying precocity which Edwards' acute dialectic of the feelings revealed in the children who came under his observation during the emotional strain of the Great Awakening. She suggests, even more directly, James' *What Maisie Knew,* though it is typical of the later writer's refinement of skill and sophistication that he would set himself the complicated problem of having both parents divorced and married again, of making the child the innocent meeting ground for a liaison between the stepparents, and of confining his report on the situation entirely to what could be glimpsed through the child's inscrutable eyes.

The symbolical intricacies of *The Scarlet Letter* open out on every fresh examination of the book, since there is hardly a scene where there are not to be found some subsidiary correspondences like those presented by the stream of separation, which just failed to carry with it the token of Hester's miserable past that she had tried in vain to fling from her. Again, the forest itself, with its straggling path, images to Hester "the moral wilderness in which she had so long been wandering"; and while describing it Hawthorne may have taken a glance back at Spenser's Wood of Errour. The clue to the success or failure of such analogies seems to consist in the measure of sound doctrine, or of imaginative fitness, or of both, which lies behind them. When they require the first and are without it, the result can be as mawkish as when Kenyon's anxious eyes followed the flight of doves upward from Hilda's deserted window, in the hope that "he might see her gentle and sweet face shining down upon him, midway towards heaven, as if she had flown thither for a day or two, just to visit her kindred, but had been drawn earthward again by the spell of unacknowledged love." It is embarrassing even to quote such a sentence, which, however, would undoubtedly have pleased Mrs. Hawthorne, whom her husband sometimes called his "Dove." But having made

out a case for Pearl, who, judging from other critics, may well be the
most unpopular little girl in fiction, it seemed only fair to present
Hawthorne at his worst.

His usually firm moral perception is vitiated very rarely by such
overtones of the era of *Godey's Lady's Book* and the genteel female.
His occasional extreme lapses from imaginative fitness seem even less
necessary. It is impossible to see on what basis he could have thought
it effective to remark that Judge Pyncheon's excessive warmth of
manner, as he walked through the town just before the election for
governor, required, "such, at least, was the rumor about town, an
extra passage of the watercarts . . . in order to lay the dust occa-
sioned by so much extra sunshine." There is no lack here of Hawthorne's shrewd observation of the Judge's sinister hypocrisy; and it
is conceivable, that if this remark had been phrased as a gibe by
some corner-store philosopher, its Yankee wryness might have succeeded. But woven as it is into the sober texture of Hawthorne's expo-
sition, it seems the almost perfect instance of Coleridge's statement
that the images of fancy "have no connexion natural or moral, but
are yoked together . . . by means of some accidental coincidence."
The way that Hawthorne's intrusive notion robs his narrative of all
sustained illusion at this point is the kind of thing James objected
to most. James insisted that the creator must regard his creation seri-
ously, that he must respect its life with the strictest detachment, and
keep out all traces of his own irrelevant comments on his characters.
These convulsive outbreaks of Hawthorne's fancy might be attributed
to the fact that he felt such an irresistible compulsion to look for
correspondences that he could not check himself even when he turned
up bad ones. His lack of a critical audience is again telling at this
point, as is his sense of the difficulties he had to overcome if his
imagination was to flow freely.

The ideal surroundings that he described for starting his imagination off enter again and again into its most successful products. He
reiterated, in a sentence in *The Snow-Image* that Melville marked, his
belief that the moon creates, "like the imaginative power, a beautiful
strangeness in familiar objects." In some of his pale demonstrations
of that truth he may seem merely to bear out another remark, which
can be turned devastatingly against him, that "feminine achievements
in literature" are so many "pretty fancies of snow and moonlight."
Yet it is also true that an extraordinary number of his major scenes
are played out under these rays. Or rather, the light does not remain
a dramatic property, but becomes itself a central actor. Such is the
case with the meteoric exhalations that harrow Dimmesdale with the
thought that knowledge of his hidden guilt is spread over the whole
broad heavens; and an even more dynamic role is played by the rising

moon during Judge Pyncheon's night watch, since, as it fingers its way through the windows, it is the only living thing in the room. And simply to mention, out of many more, the two most effectively presented crises in the other romances, we remember the midnight stream from which the dead-white body of Zenobia is recovered; and the maddened instant when Donatello, seeing Miriam's sinister model emerging from the shadows into the moonlight, cannot resist the impulse to hurl him off the Tarpeian rock.

In all these scenes Hawthorne draws on every possible contrast between lights and darks; and the way he invariably focuses attention on the thought-burdened faces of his characters justifies the frequent comparison between his kind of scrutiny and Rembrandt's. Moreover, despite his relative ignorance of painting, he deliberately created, throughout his work, sustained landscapes of low-pitched tones to heighten the effects of his foreground. He generally visualized his outdoor scenes in neutral "gray and russet," against which he projected such symbols as the brilliant crimson and purple blossoms that hang over the fountain in Rappaccini's garden, and hide deadly poison in their beauty. Or, again at night, the dark woods on the mountain side, where the final agony of Ethan Brand is enacted, are shot through not only by occasional moonbeams, but by streaks of firelight from the limeburner's roaring furnace. More complex than this effect, or that whereby the tragedy of Ilbrahim is begun in lingering twilight and ended on a night of violent storm, is the continual manipulation of the lighting in both *The Scarlet Letter* and *The House of the Seven Gables*. From the opening description of the elm-clustered old house, the sense that "the shadow creeps and creeps, and is always looking over the shoulder of the sunshine" on the great vertical dial on one of the gables is raised to the level of a central theme, for it symbolizes how the actions of the fragile present are oppressed with the darkness of the past. At the very start of *The Scarlet Letter* Hawthorne calls it "the darkening close of a tale of human frailty and sorrow, and in nearly every scene the somber values are underscored. For instance, the minister and Hester are made to meet in "the gray twilight" of the forest; and the single "flood of sunshine" in the book, which Hawthorne emphasizes by using these words as the title of the chapter, falls first on Hester in her moment of release, and then is shifted, like a spotlight, to the figure of the child at the brook. Calling attention thus to these devices makes them sound more theatrical than they are in their subdued operation; and one of the most subtle effects of the tragedy derives from the way in which the words "shadowy" and "shadowlike" are reiterated in the closing pages as a means of building up to the final sentence. This sentence describes how the heraldic device of the letter, which was carved even on Hester's gravestone, might serve

—through its dramatic contrast of a sable field with the A, gules—as a motto for the whole legend, "so somber is it, and relieved only by one ever-glowing point of light gloomier than the shadow."

Irony

Richard Harter Fogle: From *Hawthorne's Fiction: The Light and the Dark*

The intensity of *The Scarlet Letter,* at which Hawthorne himself was dismayed, comes from concentration, selection, and dramatic irony. The concentration upon the central theme is unremitting. The tension is lessened only once, in the scene in the forest, and then only delusively, since the hope of freedom which brings it about is quickly shown to be false and even sinful. The characters play out their tragic action against a background in itself oppressive—the somber atmosphere of Puritanism. Hawthorne calls the progression of the story "the darkening close of a tale of human frailty and sorrow." Dark to begin with, it grows steadily deeper in gloom. The method is almost unprecedentedly selective. Almost every image has a symbolic function; no scene is superfluous. One would perhaps at times welcome a loosening of the structure, a moment of wandering from the path. The weedy grassplot in front of the prison; the distorting reflection of Hester in a breastplate, where the Scarlet Letter appears gigantic; the tapestry of David and Bathsheba on the wall of the minister's chamber; the little brook in the forest; the slight malformation of Chillingworth's shoulder; the ceremonial procession on election day—in every instance more is meant than meets the eye.

The intensity of *The Scarlet Letter* comes in part from a sustained and rigorous dramatic irony, or irony of situation. This irony arises naturally from the theme of "secret sin," or concealment. "Show freely of your worst," says Hawthorne; the action of *The Scarlet Letter* arises from the failure of Dimmesdale and Chillingworth to do so. The minister hides his sin, and Chillingworth hides his identity. This concealment affords a constant drama. There is the irony of Chapter III, "The Recognition," in which Chillingworth's ignorance is suddenly and blindingly reversed. Separated from his wife by many vicissitudes, he comes upon her as she is dramatically exposed to public infamy. From his instantaneous decision, symbolized by the lifting of his finger to his lips to hide his tie to her, he precipitates the further irony of his sustained hypocrisy.

In the same chapter Hester is confronted with her fellow adulterer, who is publicly called upon to persuade her as her spiritual guide to reveal his identity. Under the circumstances the situation is highly charged, and his words have a double meaning—one to the onlookers, another far different to Hester and the speaker himself. "If thou feelest it to be for thy soul's peace, and that thy earthly punishment will therefore be made more effectual to salvation, I charge thee to speak out the name of thy fellow-sinner and fellow-sufferer!"

From this scene onward Chillingworth, by living a lie, arouses a constant irony, which is also an ambiguity. With a slight shift in emphasis all his actions can be given a very different interpretation. Seen purely from without, it would be possible to regard him as completely blameless. Hester expresses this ambiguity in Chapter IV, after he has ministered to her sick baby, the product of her faithlessness, with tenderness and skill. " 'Thy acts are like mercy,' said Hester, bewildered and appalled. 'But thy words interpret thee as a terror!' " Masquerading as a physician, he becomes to Dimmesdale a kind of attendant fiend, racking the minister's soul with constant anguish. Yet outwardly he has done him nothing but good. " 'What evil have I done the man?' asked Roger Chillingworth again. 'I tell thee, Hester Prynne, the richest fee that ever physician earned from monarch could not have bought such care as I have wasted on this miserable priest!' " Even when he closes the way to escape by proposing to take passage on the same ship with the fleeing lovers, it is possible to consider the action merely friendly. His endeavor at the end to hold Dimmesdale back from the saving scaffold is from one point of view reasonable and friendlike, although he is a devil struggling to snatch back an escaping soul. "All shall be well! Do not blacken your fame, and perish in dishonor! I can yet save you! Would you bring infamy on your sacred profession?" Only when Dimmesdale has successfully resisted does Chillingworth openly reveal his purposes. With the physician the culminating irony is that in seeking to damn Dimmesdale he has himself fallen into damnation. As he says in a moment of terrible self-knowledge, "A mortal man, with once a human heart, has become a fiend for his especial torment!" The effect is of an Aristotelian reversal, where a conscious and deep-laid purpose brings about totally unforeseen and opposite results. Chillingworth's relations with Dimmesdale have the persistent fascination of an almost absolute knowledge and power working their will with a helpless victim, a fascination which is heightened by the minister's awareness of an evil close beside him which he cannot place. "All this was accomplished with a subtlety so perfect that the minister, though he had constantly a dim perception of some evil influence watching over him, could never gain a knowledge of its actual nature." It is a classic situation wrought out to its fullest potentialities, in which the reader cannot help sharing the perverse pleasure of the villain.

From the victim's point of view the irony is still deeper, perhaps because we can participate still more fully in his response to it. Dimmesdale, a "remorseful hypocrite," is forced to live a perpetual lie in public. His own considerable talents for self-torture are supplemented by the situation as well as by the devoted efforts of Chillingworth. His knowledge is an agony. His conviction of sin is in exact relationship to the reverence in which his parishioners hold him. He grows pale and meager—it is the asceticism of a saint on earth; his effectiveness as a minister grows with his despair; he confesses the truth in his sermons, but transforms it "into the veriest falsehood" by the generality of his avowal and merely increases the adoration of his flock; every effort deepens his plight, since he will not—until the end—make the effort of complete self-revelation. His great election-day sermon prevails through anguish of heart; to his listeners divinely inspired, its power comes from its undertone of suffering, "the complaint of a human heart, sorrowladen, perchance guilty, telling its secret, whether of guilt or sorrow, to the great heart of mankind. . . ." While Chillingworth at last reveals himself fully, Dimmesdale's secret is too great to be wholly laid bare. His utmost efforts are still partially misunderstood, and "highly respectable witnesses" interpret his death as a culminating act of holiness and humility.

Along with this steady irony of situation there is the omnipresent irony of the hidden meaning. The author and the reader know what the characters do not. Hawthorne consistently pretends that the coincidence of the action or the image with its significance is merely fortuitous, not planned, lest the effect be spoiled by overinsistence. In other words, he attempts to combine the sufficiently probable with the maximum of arrangement. Thus the waxing and waning of sunlight in the forest scene symbolize the emotions of Hester and Dimmesdale, but we accept this coincidence most easily if we can receive it as chance. Hawthorne's own almost amused awareness of his problem helps us to do so. Yet despite the element of play and the deliberate self-deception demanded, the total effect is one of intensity. Hawthorne is performing a difficult feat with sustained virtuosity in reconciling a constant stress between naturally divergent qualities.

The character of Pearl illuminates this point. Pearl is pure symbol, the living emblem of the sin, a human embodiment of the Scarlet Letter. Her mission is to keep Hester's adultery always before her eyes, to prevent her from attempting to escape its moral consequences. Pearl's childish questions are fiendishly apt; in speech and in action she never strays from the control of her symbolic function; her dress and her looks are related to the letter. When Hester casts the letter away in the forest, Pearl forces her to reassume it by flying into an uncontrollable rage. Yet despite the undeviating arrangement of every circumstance which surrounds her, no single action of hers is ever incredible or inconsistent with the conceivable actions of any child under the same conditions. Given the central improbability of her undeviating purposiveness, she is as lifelike as the brilliantly drawn children of Richard Hughes's *The Innocent Voyage*.

AMBIGUITY

Hyatt H. Waggoner: From "Art and Belief"

The "ambiguity device," isolated and discussed so well years ago by Matthiessen, is . . . no mere "device" but an expression in technical terms of the essential condition of Hawthorne's belief. It is a method of blurring the clear eye, of refusing to specify how literally something should be taken, of believing in Providence while not pretending to understand its machinery. It is a method, we may say, of avoiding clarity—but the kind of clarity that is avoided is the kind Hawthorne thought either specious or irrelevant. Something supernatural seemed to have occurred; a natural explanation, or several natural explanations, could be given. But would the explanation, even if we could be sure it were true, render void the religious significance of the strange event? It is easy to imagine Hawthorne writing— in fact, he *should* have written, though I cannot recall that he ever did—"Whether Adam lived or no. . . ."

If, as I have argued, the shaping force behind Hawthorne's art is the special character of his religious belief, it is not surprising that the so-called ambiguity device should be one of the most characteristic features of his writing and that a more generalized ambiguity should be so typical of it. For Hawthorne's religious belief was existentially oriented, not institutional or traditional. He found in his own *experience* reason for looking at life as the "old time" writers had, reason for believing the Scriptures would never be destroyed by the bonfires of reform. But religious experience—not doctrine or dogma, but experience—is always, and necessarily, ambiguous. Did the god speak

From *"Art and Belief,"* by *Hyatt H. Waggoner, in* Hawthorne Centenary Essays, *ed. Roy Harvey Pearce. Copyright © 1964 by the Ohio State University Press. All rights reserved. Reprinted by permission of the author, the editor, and the publisher.*

or did we merely imagine his voice? If he did really speak, it is clear
that only the prepared, the imaginative ear could receive the words.
It is possible to argue that only the faithful saw the risen Christ without intending to impugn the reality of the Resurrection.

The decision as to which is the true dream and which the false
must be made by the individual in the depths of his inwardness.
Hawthorne was not without his commitments; and in some areas of
thought he was willing to declare them, preferably in allegorical form.
But on matters closest to his heart, he was either unable to attain
commitment or reluctant to declare his commitments propositionally.
His ambiguity, whether inseparable from the greatness of his finest
writing or the mere idiosyncrasy it becomes in his poorest, is a translation of this aspect of his belief into art.

DICHOTOMY

Donald A. Ringe: From "Hawthorne's Psychology of the Head and the Heart"

As Matthiessen points out, the head and the heart may be called
respectively thought and emotion, or perhaps reason and passion. To
a certain extent, the heart may be equated with nature and the head
with art, that is, intellectual activity in philosophy, art, or science. In
other words, the head is that quality which raises men above the level
of animals. We must not assume that Hawthorne placed his entire
faith in either head or heart; rather, both are necessary elements that
must be present in every man. Nor can we assume that either is inherently good or bad. Hawthorne often refers to the heart as a foul
cavern,[1] and the dangers of too great a reliance on the heart alone
are exemplified in the character of Hollingsworth in *The Blithedale
Romance*.[2] The head, however, is inherently no better. The cold,

---

*Reprinted by permission of the Modern Language Association from "Hawthorne's
Psychology of the Head and Heart" by Donald A. Ringe*. Publications of the Modern Language Association, *LXV (March, 1950), 121, 124-25. Copyright © 1950 by
the Modern Language Association.*

[1] See the conclusion of "Earth's Holocaust," *Works*, Riverside edition, 13 vols.
(Boston: Houghton, Mifflin, 1883), II, 455. This edition will hereafter be referred to
as *Works*, and documentation in my text will be to volumes and pages in this
edition. See also Randall Stewart, ed. *The American Notebooks* (New Haven: Yale
University Press, 1932), p. 98, for a long passage in which Hawthorne describes the
heart as a cavern containing several levels of good and evil, the greatest good being
deepest. In his footnote to the passage, Stewart cites passages from the *Works* in
which the heart is compared to a cavern.

[2] Hawthorne stresses the point that Hollingsworth's finest gift was his great heart,

speculative, intellectual man commits a sin of isolation which must eventually destroy him. Coverdale in *Blithedale* and Holgrave in *The House of the Seven Gables* are good examples. Coverdale's prying interest in other people's hearts almost dehumanizes him,[3] and Holgrave's inward-looking intellectual attitude almost destroys his heart.[4] . . .

This romance [*The Scarlet Letter*] develops the theme of the effect of evil upon men, and Hawthorne explores the possible solutions to the problem of human life by making use of the psychology of the head and heart. The Puritan society is an evil one—a society which collectively has committed the sins of Ego and Pride. Mistress Hibbins, the town witch, notes the evil that is present, and the egocentric self-satisfaction of the old matrons at the scaffold scene substantiates this fact. If further proof is needed, one may consider the Puritan ministers, whose intellectual development makes them incapable of sitting in honest judgment on a woman's heart.[5]

In this society, Hawthorne places three characters who represent three of several possibilities for action in the evil world. It must be noted that none of the three characters represents the head or heart in complete isolation; rather, all illustrate the two in conflict.

but since it overbalances the head, the reformer is somehow incomplete. Because he lacks controlling intellect, Hollingsworth's heart is destroyed as philanthropy becomes his one "ruling passion, in one exclusive channel" (*Works*, V, 595).

[3] He says, "That cold tendency, between instinct and intellect, which made me pry with a speculative interest into people's passions and impulses, appeared to have gone far towards unhumanizing my heart" (*Works*, V, 495).

[4] The inward-looking tendency is objectified by Holgrave's interest in daguerreotypes and the "Alice Story," and in his temptation to violate the sanctity of Phoebe's soul with mesmerism.

[5] It would, perhaps, not be unfair to say that here, as in "The May-Pole of Merry Mount" and "The Gentle Boy," the Puritans represent the head divorced to a large extent from the heart.

ARCHETYPE

William Bysshe Stein: From *Hawthorne's Faust*

On the basis of this analysis of *The Scarlet Letter* it appears that a fluid conception of the Faust myth is the dynamic principle of

From Hawthorne's Faust *by William Bysshe Stein. Gainesville: University of Florida Press, 1953, pp. 121-22. Copyright © 1953 by University of Florida Press. Reprinted by permission.*

composition ruling Hawthorne's creative imagination. Motivating most of the action in the novel is a versatile Faustian devil whose repertory of tricks derives from the Faustian drama and the Faustian Gothic romance. As Hawthorne manipulates the controlling idea, he endows each of his main characters with an aim in life that falls into the pattern of universal human experience. His portrayal of Chillingworth as a Puritan Faust who is victimized by a hereditary interest in sin elevates the latter's fate to a plane of numbing pathos and tragedy. In depicting Hester as a Fausta, Hawthorne separates her from the ordinary romantic heroine accidentally entangled in a net of evil. Her desperate efforts as a Faustian tempter are designed to express the eternal philosophy of womanhood: consistent with her maternal instincts, a woman's destiny is linked firmly with her desire to attain happiness for herself, her children, and her mate. In terms of the variant of the Faust myth, assigning to Dimmesdale the character of a lascivious monk. Hawthorne, with poetic justice that betrays his true feelings about the minister, rewards the latter's ignominious spiritual hypocrisy and moral cowardice. And by recourse to another Faustian phenomenon, Hawthorne ennobles Pearl's struggle to achieve identity in the human family.

The dramatic device of archetypal ritual in the Faust myth, the selling of the soul to the devil, provides Hawthorne with an operational symbol that enables him to analyze vividly the spiritual quandaries of his actors. This symbol effectively enlarges the experiences of the characters beyond the historical theater of Puritan times. Its associations embrace the whole complex of human desires that have given to man's life a deep significance and purpose. Hawthorne's Satan is not the principle of evil in Calvinistic theology; he is the dark fatality that eternally works in the affairs of humans who have trespassed into ethically uncharted domains of the intellect and the spirit. Only by conquering this evil which is compounded of the only two worlds man can know, the inner world of the soul and the outer of human activity, can the individual confront bravely the tragic discipline of his existence. With such implications underlying the structure of *The Scarlet Letter,* the novel assumes a greater importance than has hitherto been assigned to it in the history of American letters.

THE RANGE OF INTERPRETATIONS

The Scarlet Letter
and Its Modern
Critics

by Charles Child Walcutt

Casting about for an image that would express my sense of the relation of *The Scarlet Letter* to the body of criticism that has grown up around it, I thought of a small, one-story delicatessen in Manhattan that stands between the masses of a big hotel and a tall office building. If one were to look out from the thirtieth floor of the skyscraper he would see the hotel across a narrow airway, but if he looked down I suspect that he would not see the little delicatessen at all, for what seems to be at the foot of a skyscraper as one looks down from it turns out in fact to be a block away. This image encourages whimsical elaboration. Hawthorne himself might suggest that in the delicatessen one finds hot pastrami sandwiches and other life-giving foods, in spite of its being shut away from the sun by those remorseless towers of steel and concrete. He might also indicate that the little building has stood there a good deal longer than its great neighbors; but he could certainly not guarantee that it would outlive them, and so there the image fails.

The Scarlet Letter will outlast its critics, for it is not a book that has ever required blood transfusions from fat literary histories or that has been brought back to life by a devoted coterie with artificial respiration. Nor, to be sure, has it been maintained in a broth and forcibly fed to generations of reluctant doctoral candidates. No doubt all of us have read it more than once, with a deepening sense of its

From Nineteenth-Century Fiction, *VII, 251-64. Copyright © 1953 by The Regents of the University of California. Reprinted by permission of The Regents.*

greatness; and there are few writings in the body of our literature for which a summary of plot would be more entirely supererogatory.

Yet in reading through some dozens of books and articles in which *The Scarlet Letter* is discussed, I have found that most of them do tell its story over again in great detail and that in a substantial majority of these the space devoted to summary and to what I should call appreciation considerably exceeds the space devoted to explication. And whereas nearly every critic agrees that *The Scarlet Letter* is a very great work, it sustains a suprising variety of interpretations. I propose now to classify these various readings, as I have found them, to inquire how far they are justified by Hawthorne's words, and to consider whether their range and variety are due to some fundamental ambiguity in *The Scarlet Letter* or to the prepossessions of its readers.

At one end of the scale is the orthodox Christian, or perhaps it should be called the orthodox Puritan reading, which finds the central motive of the book in the idea that sin is permanently warping. If sin is permanently warping, the effect of Hester's and Dimmesdale's sin will prevail in everything they do thereafter. The soul of man being fallen, and the corrupt mind and will having been partly the cause and partly the result of that fall, it would follow that the mind brooding upon its error could not work its way through to a clear understanding of man's place in relation to God and Revelation. These matters are, according to the Puritan code, accessible to the clear spirit of the elect through faith but never to the mere rational intelligence. And the sin which Hester and Dimmesdale have committed will release evils in their natures which will never be entirely eradicated or forgiven. Sin plants a seed within them which grows into further evil. It may not grow like the green bay tree, but it will grow and it will not die. We love the characters who sin from the heart—Hester, Miriam, Zenobia, and Donatello; we sometimes respect or pity those possessed by pride, like Ethan Brand, Rappaccini, and Aylmer; but we hate or despise Chillingworth, Coverdale, and Wakefield. According to this reading the book is a tragedy almost in the Greek manner, for sin is ubiquitous and the reader would not view the downfall of other sinners with any complacent self-righteousness.

A major variant of this orthodox reading discovers the meaning of *The Scarlet Letter* in the concept of the Fortunate Fall, which acknowledges the reality of sin but considers it the source of wisdom and spiritual enlightenment. Hester and Dimmesdale not only expiate their sins but through them achieve wisdom, self-knowledge, spiritual powers—in short, greatness—which repay their sufferings. The Fortunate Fall reading expresses a tragic rather than a strictly orthodox view of man, for whereas the orthodox is concerned with absolute sin and its just consequences, *Felix Culpa* sees man in an evil world in which he can win greatness only through suffering. To clarify, I should add that the orthodox reading sees the tragedy in the action; whereas the Fortunate Fall reading finds it in the very essence of man's relation to the universe—his tragic plight. Less extreme versions than the one I have just described read the story in terms of redemption or purgation, acknowledging that blest spirits like Priscilla and Hilda cannot know sin but finding Hawthorne's sympathies with Hester, Miriam, and Zenobia.

Romantic readings rest on the premise that society is guilty of punishing individuals who have responded to a natural urge. No absolute sin has been committed by Hester and Dimmesdale; society has "sinned" against nature. Man is good; institutions are bad because they thwart nature. From this premise one may investigate the perversion or deterioration of the natural good in Hester and Dimmesdale through the *sense* of sin which society forces upon them. Or one may see Hester at least as living a heroic but tragic defiance of society's code, finally defeated not by any sort of inner failure but by the misfortune of Chillingworth's discovery of the planned escape or by the minister's having been tormented until he has not strength left to act for his own good. Admiring individual defiance, the romantic reader dwells upon the intellectual and spiritual growth of the protagonists and deplores the depths to which Chillingworth sinks.

I designate a fourth reading transcendental, using the term in a sense that I shall distinguish from my use of romantic, for of course transcendentalism is generally considered an area of romanticism. The transcendental reading is identified by the assertion that "the sin of Hester and Arthur is of no importance in itself"; it is either the consequences of their adultery or what follows it that matters, namely the concealment of the sin, or, to put it more specifically, the failure of self-reliance in the lovers' not being true to themselves. This is a sin against the soul, not a sin of passion or a culpable disregard of the community, but a failure of self-trust. I use Emerson's phrases because these readings usually do so. The transcendental reading balances between the orthodox idea of absolute sin and the romantic denial of it, for although it scorns the idea of a sin of passion and rejects the stubborn mores of the community, it does judge the lovers guilty of sin in not being true to themselves.

Finally, there are relativist readings of *The Scarlet Letter* which concentrate upon the psychological implications of the sense of guilt. They are not interested in sin as a fact but as an element which may function to disturb the individual's psychic balance. They study

how the sense of sin affects the personality. I call them relativist because they affirm that sin depends upon what the character thinks
is sinful, not on an absolute moral law.

Before speaking of particular critics, I offer three conclusions which
underlie what I shall have to say: the five readings I have defined
all presume to represent Hawthorne's intention in *The Scarlet Letter;*
not every critic hews to a single line of interpretation; and some
critics find inconsistency in Hawthorne, whereas others disagree with
or disapprove of the meaning which they find him attributing to
his action.

The firmest orthodox reading is by Austin Warren. He says that
Hawthorne was a Puritan, that he believed in sin and predestination
and like a true Puritan did not find these concepts incompatible.[1]
"Sin," he writes, "may be forgiven by God; softened by penitence; still
its stains persist; and its permanent effect is not educative but warping." [2] Hawthorne, he says, rejects Hester's romantic assertion that
"what we did had a consecration of its own" by describing the moral
wilderness in which she had wandered, taught much amiss by Shame,
Despair, and Solitude.[3] Mr. Warren does not waver an inch from this
line. Whether the sin be of pride or sensuality, its effects are similar:
the sin of passion sets the mind apart and adrift, whereas the sin
of pride dries up the well of brotherhood.

Frederic Carpenter finds Hawthorne pointing in the first half of
his story toward a transcendental meaning but failing in conviction
or courage and ending with pessimistic orthodoxy.[4] Newton Arvin, on
the other hand, seems to shift his ground. He begins his analysis of
The Scarlet Letter with the orthodox reading that "Dimmesdale's
nature, like Hester's, is finally perverted and vitiated by the central
falsity of his life. His refined spirituality becomes the instrument
for a diseased self-persecution: his spiritual insight turns into a loathsome apprehension of the evil in other men's breasts. As he returns
through the town after his interview with Hester in the forest, Dimmesdale is tempted at every step to perpetrate some monstrous im-
propriety of speech or act—the symbol of a moral sense gone hopelessly awry." [5] But he finally accepts Chillingworth's speech about Fate
—"It has all been a dark necessity. Ye . . . are not sinful, save in a
kind of typical illusion; neither am I fiend-like,"—and objects to the
fact that this thesis deprives the characters of free will and so limits
their vitality and verisimilitude. "Hawthorne," he writes, "preferred to

---

[1] *Nathaniel Hawthorne: Representative Selections* (New York, 1934), p. xxv.
[2] *Ibid.*, p. xxix.
[3] *Ibid.*, p. xxxiv.
[4] "Scarlet A Minus," *College English*, V (January 1944).
[5] *Hawthorne* (Boston, 1929), p. 190.

think of personal tragedy as the product of mysterious agencies outside the personality." [6] Thus, when Mr. Arvin looks into the characters, he sees them as destroyed by the effect of sin. When he looks at them theoretically, he finds them paper-thin puppets acting out a theory of Fate which he rejects. He rejects the idea that sin is permanently warping because he rejects the philosophy and the characterization which make Fate dominant. If the characters had enough free will to be convincing as personalities, they would not sin or, sinning, they would be able to redeem themselves. From this romantic position Mr. Arvin rejects the meaning which he reads in the story.

Donald Ringe works out an interesting Fortunate Fall reading turning on the idea that the human problem lies in the balance of head and heart (or mind and emotion). People with the right balance lose themselves in the great mass of humanity. Those with an unbalance either commit the unpardonable sin of pride and isolation, and there rest, or through sin and isolation achieve greatness. Hester begins with too much heart and commits a sin of passion, but in isolation her mind develops until *it* predominates. "The price of her new intelligence of heart and head is isolation. . . . Through her sin, Hester rises to a greater height than she could ever have attained without her fall, remorse, and long penance." [7] Dimmesdale, though he sins from the heart, is really a creature of the head, and he is isolated from humanity until his heart is opened by his sin. Concealment then brings on a new isolation, he falls a second time when he plans to escape with Hester, "but this time the fall has a beneficent effect," [8] for he achieves supreme knowledge and insight into man and evil, and his final sermon is controlled by the heart. "Thus Dimmesdale," he concludes, "achieves the highest moral triumph that man is capable of," [9] although the "ideal solution rests in Hester," who returns finally to the colony and reminds people of the omnipresence of sin. "The noblest qualities of heart and mind, true and profound insight into the problem of human existence," concludes Mr. Ringe, are attained only through sin.[10] In an evil world, "it is only in the Hester Prynnes . . . that gradual and perhaps continuing moral progress for man can be hoped for or sought." [11] "Hawthorne intended . . . to show that man must fall if he is to rise to heights above the normal level of men." [12]

[6] *Ibid.*, p. 218.
[7] "Hawthorne's Psychology of the Head and Heart," *PMLA*, LXV (March 1950), 125.
[8] *Ibid.*, p. 129
[9] *Ibid.*, p. 130.
[10] *Ibid.*, p. 132.
[11] *Ibid.*, p. 130.
[12] *Ibid.*, p. 132.

For resolutely romantic readings, I turn to Lloyd Morris and Ludwig Lewisohn. Mr. Morris says there was "ample cause for the orthodox to be disconcerted by *The Scarlet Letter*. . . . [Hawthorne's] romance portrayed . . . impartially and objectively . . . the consequences of what society calls sin." [13] "He had not condemned either Hester Prynne or Arthur Dimmesdale for their sin; their love, having had a consecration of its own, never caused them repentance. Hester's elaboration of the badge of her shame into a beautiful emblem was paralleled, in her life, by the elaboration of the sin into nothing but beauty. Because of her sin she achieved a moral career . . . [and] became more loving, more comprehending, and intellectually more emancipated than if she had not sinned." [14] "The novel . . . challenged society's right to restrict the freedom of individual passion. But its import was even more radical. It raised the question whether sin itself, rather than the repentance of sin, is not the source of the highest good." It "justified the self-reliant individual and expressed [Hawthorne's] contempt for the society which hedges that individual about with conventions devoid of spiritual validity." [15] Mr. Lewisohn sees in the novel the tragedy of a great spirit destroyed by the world. He describes Hester as rising above her Puritan environment to the knowledge that her adultery had a consecration of its own. "And so it is acceptable to the imagination and the moral sensibility that Hester persuades Dimmesdale to flee with her, and equally that their flight is frustrated only and again by that old man. . . ." [16] In spite of the tragic ending, Hester and Arthur triumph "over the evil rooted in the hearts and embodied in the institutions of men." [17] Of guilt and sin, which Lewisohn says control Hawthorne's genius, he finds this book alone to be free! This is indeed a long way from the orthodox readings.

Romantic readings will not consider sin as sin but blame society for its persecution of the self-reliant individual; they do not see that for Hawthorne the social consequences of sin were a part of its punishment.

F. O. Matthiessen speaks of Hester's sin as having a consecration of its own, and of "her purgatorial course through the book." [18] He says Hawthorne "shared the belief that only those who can suffer intensely are fully alive, since, as he said, there are 'spiritual depths

[13] *The Rebellious Puritan: Portrait of Mr. Hawthorne* (New York, 1927), p. 229.
[14] *Ibid.*
[15] *Ibid.*
[16] *Expression in America* (New York, 1932), p. 181.
[17] *Ibid.*, p. 182.
[18] *American Renaissance* (New York, 1941), p. 276.

which no other spell can open.' " [19] This romantic reading is documented with the quotation, " 'the only truth' that continued to give the minister 'a real existence on this earth was the anguish in his inmost soul.' " But this anguish is something quite different in its context, which reads as follows:

> To the untrue man, the whole universe is false,—it is impalpable,—it shrinks to nothing within his grasp. And he himself, in so far as he shows himself in a false light, becomes a shadow, or, indeed, ceases to exist. The only truth that continued to give Mr. Dimmesdale a real existence on this earth was the anguish in his inmost soul.[20]

Here is no strength through suffering, but the anguish of a man who has lost touch with all reality but his ghastly thoughts, which whirl in a dark chaos of doubt, despair, and error.

Mark Van Doren finds that "Hester becomes a heroine, almost a goddess." [21] She is ancient New England's "most heroic creature." [22] Her life, "increases, not diminishes, in the bleak world whose best citizen she is"; she is the "blackest sacrifice [that Puritanism] ever offered on its altar." [23] Hawthorne "recoils from the Puritan view of sin" but presents it as a solemn fact for Hester and the people of her time. This implies that the sense of sin is a social imposition, and Mr. Van Doren comes to the romantic conclusion that "Hester's life has not been hollow, nor has her great nature been wasted." [24]

Transcendental readings seldom appear unmixed with others. G. E. Woodberry opens with the romantic reading that "Hester's punishment . . . illustrates the law's brutality . . . it is man's social way of dealing with sin, and fails because it makes no connection with the soul; the victim rises above it, is emancipated from its ideas, transforms the symbol of disgrace into a message of mercy to all who suffer, and annuls the gross sentence by her own higher soul-power." [25] Yet Woodberry acknowledges the serious effects of sin, which leaves implacable evil in the soul, and becomes clearly transcendental in his conclusion that "it was not a sin against law that had been committed; it was a sin against the soul, and the sin against the soul lay in the lack of confession." [26] Percy Boynton echoes these sentiments thirty-five years later: "As the tale progresses Hester triumphs, regains her

[19] *Ibid.*, p. 344.
[20] *The Scarlet Letter*, Chapter XI.
[21] *Hawthorne* (New York, 1950), p. 147.
[22] *Ibid.*, p. 151.
[23] *Ibid.*, p. 152.
[24] *Ibid.*, p. 153.
[25] *Nathaniel Hawthorne* (New York, 1902), pp. 193-94.
[26] *Ibid.*, p. 198.

position in the community . . . plans to fly . . . unrebuked by the author-moralist. And the unforgivable sin becomes not the lovers' momentary surrender to passion, but the minister's prolonged and cowardly violation of his own integrity." [27]

Romantic and transcendental readings are both monistic in denying that there is any marked breach between natural impulse and moral good, but the latter affirms a universal order against which the individual may sin by a failure to obey his intuition of good. Relativist readings imply this monism, but interest themselves primarily in the psychological balance of the individual. Thus, Herbert Gorman says that "Hawthorne is not concerned with sin as sin. That, curiously enough, was a mere starting point for him." [28] When Hester in the forest meeting says, "What we did had a consecration of its own," he comments: "In this flashing instant Hawthorne springs clear of all Puritan influence." [29] John C. Gerber in a complicated relativist reading stresses his belief that sin means something different to each character in the story and is to be understood only in terms of these special meanings. Hester, he says, does not sin against God, against her own nature, or against the community. She feels that she has broken the "law of order" of the universe. Later she finds that she has been "false to her own nature" [30] in concealing Chillingworth's identity from Dimmesdale. For this she repents sincerely when she reveals the truth and begs his forgiveness in the forest. Her insistence there that "what we did had a consecration of its own" justifies her adultery to herself, which is all that matters, and her plan of fleeing with Pearl and the minister is an action which is right for her; but Pearl's conduct thereafter shows that it "is no real solution"—a statement revealing absolute standards that repeatedly clash with the relativist ones in this reading. Chillingworth's standard is nature. "The main point to keep in mind is that Chillingworth never conceives of his own actions as righteous or sinful, but only as natural or unnatural." [31] His values are intellectual zeal and social harmony. His sin, as he and Hawthorne see it, is the surrender of his intellect to vengeance, for in this he is being false to his own intellectual principles. Dimmesdale sins in the silence which isolates him and drives him nearly insane; his specious confessions in his sermons and his secret penances are violations both of the natural order and of his love of truth. When Hester truly repents her deception and reveals Chillingworth's identity she brings in a climax of

[27] *Literature and American Life* (New York, 1936), p. 536.

[28] *Hawthorne: A Study in Solitude* (New York, 1927), p. 85.

[29] *Ibid.*, p. 86.

[30] "Form and Content in *The Scarlet Letter*," *New England Quarterly*, XVII (1944), 47.

[31] *Ibid.*, p. 36.

catharsis and purification by which she is "purged of stain" even though she cannot free herself from the consequences of her adultery. But Dimmesdale's decision to flee brings him into a terrible conflict between the code of nature and the moral law. The moral sense wins, he becomes truly penitent, and achieves a reunion with the good which enables him to write the election sermon, to confess, and to come at the end "into a truth relation with all the elements against which he has sinned." [32]

The discord among these interpretations of *The Scarlet Letter* may be traced to several causes. First is Hawthorne's symbolism, for his ubiquitous symbols convey meanings different from those communicated by his statements. Nature, for example, operates in the figure of the "wilderness of error" through which Hester is said to wander. Nature asserts itself in Pearl, whose wildness embodies the "freedom of a broken law." Nature originally supplies the impulse of Hester's and Arthur's sin of passion. In these and many other more explicit statements nature acts as a force contrary to the moral law. But nature through other symbols clearly shines upon and approves of Hester and her sin. Beside the prison in Chapter I, the "black flower" of society, grows the rose of love and beauty. Pearl is a rose too, and at the governor's mansion she fortifies this symbolism by crying for a red rose and refusing to be pacified. Pearl, the rose, repeatedly demands that Dimmesdale acknowledge his guilt. Nature shines in Hester's beauty and courage. And the sun of nature, most significantly, shines in blessing upon Hester when, in the forest, she takes off her cap and reveals the rich beauty of her hair. At this point Hester is not acknowledging her sin; rather she is declaring her passion again, her defiance of Puritan rule, and her eagerness to act upon her passion and flee with Dimmesdale to another community in which they can live openly together. This is utter sin, as Hawthorne clearly says, but the force of the nature symbols is to draw the reader's sympathy and make him conclude, in spite of the evidence, that the author, too, not only sympathizes with Hester's impulses but also endorses them. What is this evidence? Before the forest walk, Hester lies to Pearl about the scarlet letter. She has "never before been false to the symbol on her bosom," [33] and with this lie a "guardian spirit" forsakes her because "some new evil" has crept into her heart "or some old one had never been expelled." A moment later she speaks to Pearl with unwonted harshness and threatens to shut her in the dark closet. And in the forest meeting which follows, after seeing that Dimmesdale's ruin is the result of her concealment of Chillingworth's identity, it is in defense against his

[32] *Ibid.*, pp. 53-54.
[33] Chapter XV.

terrible accusations that she declares: "What we did had a consecration of its own." Dimmesdale then says, "Hush, Hester . . ." and "one solemn old tree groaned dolefully to another" over their lost heads, telling their sad story or foreboding "evil to come." After this, in moral darkness they determine to flee, and Hawthorne judges their decision in terms that are not ambiguous. Hester, he writes, had wandered long in a moral wilderness, estranged from human institutions, "criticizing . . . with hardly more reverence than the Indian would feel for the clerical band. . . . Shame, Despair, Solitude! These had been her teachers,—stern and wild ones,—and they had made her strong, but taught her much amiss." [34] These strong words close the paragraph in which Hester is evaluated at the moment of her great choice. Of the minister, who had been constantly in touch with truth, Hawthorne asks: "Were such a man once more to fall, what plea could be urged in extenuation of his crime? None," except "that he was broken down by long and exquisite suffering." But the suffering is the result of his sin. His decision to flee from "the heavy doom which he was now expiating" is judged in a heavy sentence: "And be the stern and sad truth spoken, that the breach which guilt has once made into the human soul is never, in this mortal state, repaired. It may be watched and guarded . . . but there is still the ruined wall, and, near it, the stealthy tread of the foe that would win over again his unforgotten triumph." [35]

The following chapter, "The Minister in a Maze," carries this judgment through by showing Dimmesdale possessed with a dozen obscene and blasphemous impulses as he walks back through the town. "At every step he was incited to do some strange, wild, wicked thing or other, with a sense that it would be at once involuntary and intentional." The acid of evil has corroded his soul and defaced his world. "This lost and desperate man," as Hawthorne calls him, is adrift without bearings.

This action and comment on the pivotal scene of the novel, wherein the sinners reveal that the breach of guilt has not been repaired, give Hawthorne's ample account of the spiritual condition of his protagonists. The flood of sunshine that bathes Hester's uncovered hair for a moment does not utter a full benediction on her sin, nor does it express the author's final comment on her moral state. But the reader whose heart inclines that way reacts to the bright nature symbol in the middle of this moral gloom and concludes that it expresses the novel's romantic meaning.

Another reason for the variety of these readings is that although Hawthorne's position is orthodox, he writes with a sympathy for his

[34] Chapter XVIII.
[35] *Ibid.*

erring characters and records their blunders with such tenderness that it is easy to believe that he intends to justify them. Early in the story, for example, one may feel such pity for Hester alone at her needle that he ignores Hawthorne's plain comment on her thoughts: "This morbid meddling of conscience with an immaterial matter betokened, it is to be feared, no genuine and steadfast penitence, but something doubtful, something that might be deeply wrong, beneath." [36] Later, in describing Hester's conduct as a sister of mercy to the dying, Hawthorne says "this might be pride, but was like humility," just as he says elsewhere that her refusal to flee from the scene of her disgrace was evidence not of true humility but of her love for Dimmesdale, and of defiance, which is another name for pride. The scarlet letter had not done its office.

Modern readers value intelligence and perceptiveness so highly that they see in Dimmesdale's tormented insights into the hearts of his parishioners signs that he has grown in spiritual strength. But Hawthorne does not say so. He says that Dimmesdale's burden of sin "kept him down on a level with the lowest. . . . But this very burden it was that gave him sympathies so intimate with the sinful brotherhood of mankind, so that his heart vibrated in unison with theirs, and received their pain into itself, and sent its own throb of pain through a thousand other hearts, in gushes of sad, persuasive eloquence." [37] He caused the virgins of his church to grow pale around him—a statement which suggests Hawthorne's notion, elaborated elsewhere, that the thoughts of the sinner can bring sin into the hearts of the guiltless. They are indeed presented sympathetically, but neither the minister's suffering nor his persuasive eloquence come from spiritual heights. They are from the depths.

Another cause of confusion, which I have not time to elaborate, is the universal impulse to participate in the life of a plotted action and to identify oneself with the characters in the center of such an action. Thousands of readers have been bloodthirsty with Richard III, murderous and terrified with Macbeth. How could they resist being sinners with Hester and Dimmesdale?

But the ultimate source of ambiguity in *The Scarlet Letter* lies in the fact that although Hawthorne firmly believes sin to be permanently warping, he does not in his heart love the Providence which ordains it thus.

[36] Chapter V.
[37] Chapter XI.

Dimmesdale's Fall

by Edward H. Davidson

In Christian doctrine, to which the New England Puritans scrupulously conformed, the Fall cannot be considered as a mere theological abstraction or as an historical event which happened in the ages long past. The Fall is an actual occurrence in the life of every Christian who, never sure of his soul, must continually remind himself, "I fell, I fall, I die daily that I may rise and live—even to fall and rise again." The Fall is, therefore, not only the possible beginning of that salvation which God alone can initiate, but the first step in self-knowledge; unless a man sees himself in his degradation, he remains a hopeless enigma even to himself. Hawthorne was well aware of this doctrine and made it one of his most mordant commentaries on humankind: the Fall is the only explanation of that bond of ignominy by which all men share a common brotherhood. It is the beginning of understanding and of what Edwards called "being"—that perception of man's "consent" to share the burden he bears with all mankind.

The narrative of the Reverend Arthur Dimmesdale in *The Scarlet Letter* is quite in keeping with the oldest and most fully authorized principles in Christian thought. His "Fall" is, to be sure, a descent from a state of apparent grace to damnation; he appears to begin in purity—he ends in corruption; he may once have been a whole man—at his death he is in spiritual disintegration. The subtlety of Hawthorne's presentation is that the minister is his own deceiver; he is that truly damned man who convinces himself at every stage of his spiritual pilgrimage that he is really "saved." More terrifying still, he is that rare man who is gifted with unusual powers of penetration into his own mind and soul—and all that he ever sees is a projection of his private universe. He moves steadily toward his doom quite unaware of where he is going. His Fall is, therefore, dire and irrefutable: by a sin of the flesh which he did not expiate, he corrupted his whole being. He becomes, at the last, his own savior and god, his own demon and

"*Dimmesdale's Fall*," by Edward H. Davidson. New England Quarterly, *XXXVI* (*September, 1963*), *358-70.* Copyright © *1963 by the* New England Quarterly. *Reprinted by permission of the* New England Quarterly *and Edward H. Davidson.*

destroyer. We might follow the stages in this Fall which a Puritan from the age of the Mathers to Edwards would well understand.[1]

Our first view of Dimmesdale gives us a hint of what seems to be his childlike credulity and simplicity; he is in the habit of treading "shadowy by-paths" and of enjoying his privacy; but when he comes forth into the light of ordinary day, he does so with "a freshness, and fragrance, and dewy purity of thought, which, as many people said, affected them like the speech of an angel." [2] His first words to Hester are an admonition that she is morally responsible for the guilty secret she is hiding; she bears a double infamy, her own and that of her partner. In his eloquent appeal that she reveal her paramour, he warns, "What can thy silence do for him . . . except . . . to add hypocrisy to sin? Heaven hath granted thee an open ignominy, that thereby thou mayest work out an open triumph over the evil within thee, and the sorrow without. Take heed how thou deniest to him . . . the bitter, but wholesome, cup that is now presented to thy lips!" It is instructive to note that Dimmesdale habitually refers to himself only in the third person when he is exploring the possibility of his own sin; he conveniently establishes an "it" and "I" congruence between his spiritual being, which remains somehow apart from this condemnation, and that other self which must accept the normal consequences of man's life.

The distinction is not only rhetorical and stylistic; it is "real," for the first true stage in Dimmesdale's downfall comes when the minister convinces himself that the body and the soul are separate, not merely as differing expressions of life, but as absolute distinctions of the human being. The sufferings and privations of one need not be the affliction of the other; body does not conform to the motions of the soul, and spirit need not agree with the behavior of the flesh. Chillingworth, who acts as chorus to the minister's degradation, very cleverly plays on

[1] The argument of this study begins with Henry James' statement that *The Scarlet Letter* is primarily the story, not of Hester Prynne, but of Dimmesdale, that "more wretched and pitiable culprit"; *Hawthorne* (New York, 1880), p. 109. It admittedly goes quite counter to most interpretations of the novel, of which the following are germane and representative: W. Stacy Johnson, "Sin and Salvation in Hawthorne," *Hibbert Journal*, L (October 1951), 39-47; Hyatt Waggoner, *Hawthorne: A Critical Study* (Cambridge, 1955), p. 143; Anne Marie McNamara, " 'The Character of Flame': The Function of Pearl in *The Scarlet Letter*," *American Literature*, XXVII (January 1956), 537-53; R. R. Male, *Hawthorne's Tragic Vision* (Austin, 1957), p. 94; Harry Levin, *The Power of Blackness* (New York, 1958), p. 76. Newton Arvin was the first to suggest that Dimmesdale was in danger of damnation; see *Hawthorne* (Boston, 1929), p. 190; and R. H. Fogle has maintained that Hawthorne "refused" to grant forgiveness to Dimmesdale at his death; see *Hawthorne's Fiction: The Light and the Dark* (Norman, 1952), pp. 107, 186.

[2] All quotations from *The Scarlet Letter* are to *The Centenary Edition of The Works of Nathaniel Hawthorne* (Ohio State University Press, 1962), Vol. I.

this casuistical point. He early perceives that Dimmesdale, "all spiritual as he seems, . . . hath inherited a strong animal nature. . . . Let us," he counsels himself, "dig a little farther in the direction of this vein!" He does so, most diabolically, by proposing to Dimmesdale the opposite view as though, by guileful indirection, he might mislead the minister into a deadly illusion. Chillingworth reasons with Dimmesdale that the split between the soul and the body only "seems"; it is not real or even true, except to the untrue man, and therefore, because flesh and spirit are really one, a "bodily disease [is] . . . but a symptom of some ailment in the spiritual part. . . . You," he says pointedly to the minister, "are he whose body is the closest conjoined, and imbued, and identified, so to speak, with the spirit whereof it is the instrument." Later he insinuatingly repeats the argument: "a sickness, a sore place, . . . in your spirit, hath immediately its appropriate manifestation in your bodily frame."

Chillingworth has penetrated more deeply than he has imagined: Dimmesdale's profoundest dread is that he may, by gesture, word, or action, reveal the guilty secret of his flesh and thereby threaten the lofty state of his soul. If Chillingworth's reasoning is correct, then indeed the corruption of the body is the corruption of the soul, and man goes his long journey to damnation. If, however, the flesh partakes only of the fleshly corruption and the soul abides in its own realm of being, then a man may say to himself that he is degraded in only one part. Jonathan Edwards' inquiries into the process of salvation, or damnation, would have found no more fitting memorial than Hawthorne's obsessed man: Dimmesdale had effected the destruction of what Edwards called "the consent of being to Being"; man is saved or damned, not by the dislodgment of one portion of his life from another, but by his knowing in all humility that what he is in his fleshly being he reflects in his soul, and the state of his spirit is manifest every instant in the outward demeanor of his daily experience.

This thought tortures Dimmesdale beyond endurance. On several occasions he tests to prove the supposition true: he pronounces from his pulpit his vile and degraded state; he confesses that he is "the worst of sinners, an abomination, a thing of unimaginable iniquity"—and the people but "reverence him the more." The supposed confession is meaningless because the words were mere utterances of breath, of the flesh; they were but "body," and thus they had no intellectual or spiritual substance; they were toys of speculation, playthings in an aimless casuistical logic.

In the secret privacy of his room, Dimmesdale has a chance further to test the validity of this haunting supposition that flesh and spirit partake of the same being and that one accords with the other. After a series of fasts and vigils, flagellations and scourgings until his flesh is bloody, Dimmesdale, as if his spirit were made hypersensitive in sympathy with his body, has visions "of diabolic shapes, that grinned and mocked," of "shining angels, who flew upward heavily," of "the dead friends of his youth, and his white-bearded father, with a saint-like frown, and his mother, turning her face away as she passed by." Last of all "glided Hester Prynne, leading along little Pearl . . . and pointing her forefinger, first, at the scarlet letter on her bosom, and then at the clergyman's own breast." Yet the terror lasts but a moment: these spectral warnings are not real, for the minister "could discern substances through their misty lack of substance, and convince himself that they were not solid in their nature, like yonder table of carved oak." The torment has passed, and Dimmesdale is all the more certain that things of the flesh are fleshly and perceptions of the soul are spiritual.

If Dimmesdale can condemn the flesh for sin and guilt of which the spirit is presumably free, he cannot escape the gnawing torment that his outward semblance of look and behavior may reveal his secret. He is brought suddenly against the probability that his features of eye and mouth have been recast in Pearl's face and that, in this most common revelation, he may be detected. "O . . . what a thought is that, and how terrible to dread it!" he cries, "that my own features were partly repeated in her face, and so strikingly that the world might see them!" The cry sounds like fatherly solicitude that the child may bear a double odium; but the appeal comes long after Dimmesdale has assured himself that his soul has been freed from the torments of the flesh. Others may suffer the ignominy of the body; he enjoys its transcendent and exquisite pain as sign of his spiritual exaltation.

The minister has convinced himself that the dislocation of soul from body is irrefutable and that the world, with its temptations and sorrows, is but the shadow of a shadow. "The only truth, that continued to give Mr. Dimmesdale a real existence on this earth," Hawthorne notes, "was the anguish in his inmost soul, and the undissembled expression of it in his aspect." He reasons with Chillingworth on a most curious, and insinuatingly wicked, argument: he suggests that the judgment on that Last Day will not be God's punishment of the damned and reward of the saved. Quite the contrary: judgment day will be the final revelation of human guilt and the opening of the mysteries of this world "merely to promote the intellectual satisfaction of all intelligent beings, who will stand waiting, on that day, to see the dark problem of his life made plain. . . . And I conceive," the minister concludes, "that the hearts holding such miserable secrets . . . will yield them up . . . not with reluctance, but with a joy unutterable." This is indeed a strange doctrine, that God is planning an intellectual and spiritual guessing game for the children of men. Dimmesdale even repeats it, in slightly variant terms suitable to the less sophisticated understandings of Hester and her child: "At the great judgment day, . . . thy mother, and thou, and I, must stand together! But the daylight of this world shall not see our meeting!" As though in heavenly dismay at this pronouncement, the meteors flash across the sky to show that the saintly Winthrop has passed from this world or, perhaps, that the farther universe does not accept this wily logic.

Dimmesdale's "Fall" is, in religious and philosophical terms, the "skeptical predicament." It is a descent into one of the most haunting and terrifying conditions of the human soul. It is the narrative of many sinners and saints, of Augustine in his despair, of Edwards in his questioning, of Pascal, all of whom used doubt as the first step toward the affirmation of belief. In the skeptical argument, which Dimmesdale follows albeit unknowingly, the believer or doubter must abjure all rational certitude that he can establish the principle of divine authority. God is, of a certainty, "God," but man's knowledge of Him cannot be based on the orderly operations of this world; rather, the principle of God must be predicated on that which is most "God," namely, a divine essence which, by virtue of its divinity, does not deign to assume earthly form nor display itself in the behavior of human or natural life. Thus flesh is separate from spirit; "essence" does not inhabit body; man lives a double life, condemned to the daily galling of his flesh and exalted, if exaltation is possible, in his spirit. Since man can struggle only feebly to overcome his fallen state, his one recourse is to live under the condemnation of the flesh and yet to seek, by direction of those ineffable signs which God does give to man, the way toward understanding and even salvation.

If Dimmesdale descends toward that place of doubt which skeptics, and saints too, have known, he never reaches that center of despair which Pascal, for one, so brilliantly revealed. Despair is the measure of a man's ignominy in his own sight and in the sight of God; it is the token of true self-awareness which nothing can appease except the full knowledge of the utter meanness and triviality of one's own soul. Dimmesdale's horrifying condemnation of his body is an outward and, for him, visible sign, not of the appropriate condemnation of the flesh which might begin the way toward enlightenment, but of the widening distance between the two sides of his being. The flagellations are to convince him that only the flesh bears the odium of Adam's primal crime; the body alone shows the hideous marks of its damnation. All the while the soul, even as the minister thinks it is freed from the infamy of its partner, is damned irrevocably. Mistress Hibbins, even before the minister's public confession, knows his state with unmatched clarity: "When the Black Man sees one of his own servants, signed and sealed, so shy of owning to the bond as is the Reverend Mr. Dimmesdale, he hath a way of ordering matters so that the mark shall be disclosed . . . to the eyes of all the world!" Dimmesdale's abject and, at the same time, self-glorifying spiritual pride has turned his whole world into a deadly illusion: "It is the unspeakable misery of a life so false as his," Hawthorne remarks, "that it steals the pith and substance out of whatever realities there are around us, and which were meant by Heaven to be the spirit's joy and nutriment. To the untrue man, the whole universe is false,—it is impalpable,—it shrinks to nothing within his grasp."

The Fall in *The Scarlet Letter* is thus in keeping with one of the main traditions in Christian thought; it is quite in accord with that central drama of the Puritan quest for self-awareness through pain and the darkness of the soul. Yet Dimmesdale undergoes a second "Fall"; it may not be suitable to the teachings of seventeenth and eighteenth century Puritan divines; it is, however, singularly apposite to the time in which the novel was written, for it is a moment in the drama of Romantic consciousness.

The skeptical predicament did not disappear when, with the closing of the seventeenth and the opening of the eighteenth centuries, men thought they could know God in the mechanism and worship divinity in the design. The valid issues of doubt, left from Hume and Berkeley and intensified by the new perils of idealistic thought from Germany, led directly to the Romantic sensibility. By means of the skeptical argument concerning the relation of the single self to the world, of the question of knowledge when "knowing" is controlled by and pertinent only to the single knower, and of the continuity of ideas which are subsumed under the special character of a man both acting and knowing, the Romantic inquiry entered that strange domain of the egocentric consciousness, the journey of the single autonomous mind, which formed the boundaries of such diverse writers as Wordsworth, Coleridge, and Carlyle, of Emerson, Thoreau, Whitman, and, later, William James. However out of keeping his place may be in such company, Dimmesdale belongs in the record of Romantic thought; he is a case in the Romantic sensibility; he is a member of that demon-driven band which includes Byron's Cain and Melville's Ahab.

The Romantic version of the Fall was quite like that other descent of the soul in Christian tradition (the very animus of Romantics like Shelley to the Christian assumption betrays the relationship). The one significant difference was that the new psychology of the Fall abandoned any formal authority or rationale of creeds, dogma, or history and made the soul's downward journey a descent into the darkness which was a necessary prologue to self-discovery. The Fall was, accordingly, not the loss of self, but only the removal of that portion of the self which must be lost or discarded in order for the self to find its true being. One "fell" that he might be freed from convention, from the entanglements of prejudice and conformity, from everything that, for Wordsworth or Thoreau, denied the self's unique character. One fell into "non-being"; one rose to "being." Carlyle's *Sartor Resartus* and Emerson's "Fate" are texts in the history of that necessary privation which must accompany the almost ecstatic loss of that encumbrance which, until one "fell," would threaten one with a greater annihilation—the wastage of the mind and soul in an inimical, a debased world.

Thus the Romantic sensibility interpreted the Fall both morally and aesthetically. Shelley's Prometheus was chained to a rock in the Caucasus for an infraction of the divine law, but his real revolt was in behalf of art and the artist who annihilates a universe that he may create a new wonder. Romantic ontology made the Fall an inevitable prelude to self-realization; it was the "noble doubt" which accompanied every moment of the inquiring spirit; it was not just one occasion in the artist's lifetime in which he "fell" and "rose"; it was, rather, a dramatic and personal necessity on each separate occasion when a work of art was undertaken. The Fall became, therefore, that necessary, obsessive moment which must precede the accomplishment of any work of art. Quite rightly the Romantic artist sought to be possessed by his "Daemon."

Dimmesdale's Fall, in the context of moral Romanticism, begins at a stage in his descent after the other and parallel Fall had already been under way. Our earliest clue is his conjecture that the confrontation of the single self and the world outside is inevitable and unceasing pain; yet that pain is the preliminary step to self-enlightenment; suffering has meaning and anguish has purpose. Dimmesdale first voices this argument when, during the interview in Governor Bellingham's mansion, Hester is found wanting in the religious instruction of her child. She appeals frantically to the minister, who speaks assuringly: "This child . . . hath come from the hand of God. . . . It was meant for a blessing. . . . It was meant, . . . as the mother herself hath told us, for a retribution too; a torture, to be felt at many an unthought of moment; a pang, a sting, an ever-recurring agony, in the midst of a troubled joy!" Pain of the body one can endure; pain of the soul is the deepest hurt of all. Yet suffering and humiliation are the only valid ways toward understanding. As if in elaboration of this argument which he has placed, quite effectively, in Hester's defense, Dimmesdale then reasons on his own situation. If he were merely a clod or a beast, then he would never have been afflicted with the pain which tortures him. Since his refinement and perceptions are the inevitable accompaniments of guilt and sorrow, then he should be willing, albeit the flesh rebels, to endure the anguish gladly. The soul's doubt and the hurt of the spirit are God's twinges. "Were I an atheist," he says, "—a man devoid of conscience,—a wretch with coarse and brutal instincts, —I might have found peace, long ere now. . . . But, as matters stand with my soul, . . . all of God's gifts that were the choicest have become the ministers of spiritual torment. . . . I am," he cries, "most miserable!" The Romantic elevation of the exquisitely tuned self seldom obtained so dire and haunting a commentary as this exaltation of a minister who had made adultery not a sin but a way toward the fullest accomplishment of the self.

Dimmesdale shapes the world into a solipsistic projection of his innermost guile and balances the universe on the pinpoint of his own unique cognition. Whatever he sees "is," and whatever he thinks becomes the truth of the absolute. He makes, at one stage of his pilgrimage, a quite subtle distinction between "penance" and "penitence." One is mere motion and gesture, the empty formalism of the hypocritical heart; the other is that profound abnegation of the soul which God requires before the sinner can be cleansed. However cogently he recognizes to what definition his own behavior conforms, Dimmesdale knows the words are but toys of speculation by which the mind can make its own truth in any way it desires. Perhaps, for the skeptic, only the Word is real after all: a word, any word can evoke a belief or call forth a thought. Yet Dimmesdale cannot escape the terrifying possibility that words may be freighted with meaning: even as he stands in the pulpit and makes open declaration of his shame and corruption, he is not quite sure but that his words may convey his inward confession. When the parishioners nod their heads and credit him with most saintly spirit, then Dimmesdale knows he is free: words are even emptier than the air which carries them.

The skeptic's and the Romantic's version of the Fall merge in one principle. The true and final damnation comes when, having chosen to descend in order that he may rise and having disjoined the several parts of his being in order that he may gain a truly unified sensibility, a man may so far widen the rifts in his consciousness that the real world becomes itself a riven and dismembered horror. Poe entered this frightening disjunction in "The Fall of the House of Usher" and in "The Raven"; and Melville sent Captain Ahab on a voyage which drove toward the obsessive and irrevocable dislodgment of the world from a man's own being. Thus the Fall turns downward with an ever-increasing acceleration and leads, not to self-abnegation and eventual regeneration, but to ultimate annihilation.

Dimmesdale's Fall along this route of the destructive consciousness

is as awesome as that of a soul plummeting through Milton's chaos to
hell. We can follow that descent because Hawthorne has carefully
charted it for us. It begins for Dimmesdale during the forest interview
when he pledges with Hester that the two would leave Boston and
thereby live for "self." Then Dimmesdale walks to the village and undergoes a sudden transformation which would delight the gloating eyes
of Satan or Chillingworth. In yielding himself "with deliberate choice"
to do that which "he knew was deadly sin," Dimmesdale finally acknowledged the long-hidden secrets of his bestial, fleshly nature. He
never had effected a separation of flesh from spirit; the wickedness of
one was the evil of the other; "the infectious poison of that sin," Hawthorne says, "[was] rapidly diffused throughout his moral system."
Dimmesdale meets one of the saintly deacons of his church and nearly
mouths some awful blasphemy; he passes "the eldest female member of
his church" and almost speaks a dreadful heresy; he hastens by "a
maiden newly won," for he can hardly keep from speaking a dreadful
obscenity. It was, Hawthorne noted, "another man" who had returned
from the forest interview. The Dimmesdale who emerged had lost hold
on reality; his "mind vibrated between two ideas; either that he had
[been] . . . only in a dream hitherto, or that he was merely dreaming
. . . now." He had gone the dire and crucial way when, by condemn-
ing the world of the actual, he was betrayed by the very bestiality he
had presumably renounced. His obsessions were not mere "dream";
they were themselves real.

Dimmesdale's fullest revelation comes at his public confession. It is
hardly a "confession" at all, but rather a triumphant display of that
egocentric conviction that man builds his universe from within. It is
as though Emerson's declarative possibility of each man's self-truth
were lit by hell fire. The confession merits careful attention. Dimmesdale's first words are not pleas for sympathy but cautions to Hester:
"The law we broke!—the sin here so awfully revealed!—let these alone
be in thy thoughts!" The minister's definition of "penitence" as opposed to "penance" is ironically appropriate. Then Dimmesdale continues: "It may be that, when we forgot our God,—when we violated
our reverence each for the other's soul,—it was thenceforth vain to
hope that we could meet hereafter, in an everlasting and pure reunion." Note the emphasis on the enclosing "we" and "our" in
Dimmesdale's shared damnation—hardly a solace for the woman who
had endured so patiently the trial of seven years.

Then occurs the most remarkable solipsistic argument of all: the
dying man's words are uttered, only to come back and turn in upon
themselves as though the Word is the soul's true currency and mortal
flesh is but the vestment of regeneration in one man's egocentric universe:

God knows; and *He* is merciful! *He* hath proved *his* mercy, most of all, in *my* afflictions. By giving *me* this burning torture to bear upon *my* breast! By sending yonder dark and terrible old man, to keep the torture always at red-heat! By bringing *me* hither, to die this depth of triumphant ignominy before the people! Had either of these agonies been wanting, *I* had been lost for ever! Praised be *his* name! *His* will be done! Farewell!

Note the measured, and arbitrarily italicized, insistence on only two beings, God and Dimmesdale. The universe is lit, in the dying man's eyes, by a light which shines only upon him; and when that light went out, only a murmur "rolled . . . heavily after the departed spirit."

Perhaps the question is meaningless: did Dimmesdale die damned or saved? Chillingworth, for one, quite obviously believed that the minister's soul had been cleansed at the last instant: the leech, "as one intimately connected with the drama of guilt and sorrow," knelt beside the dying man and "repeated more than once, . . . 'Thou hast escaped me!'" Chillingworth's revenge, as monstrous as Hamlet's aim of sending King Claudius to suffer in eternity, did fail. Yet, for all the diabolical guile he had invented, Chillingworth may have merely embellished what had already been accomplished. Dimmesdale was damned the moment he regarded himself as a particular, a destined man whose sin could ennoble and whose suffering might spiritualize the gross, earthly part. He committed himself to an irretrievable split in his life and being: the flesh he beat and denigrated as though it alone were the cancerous part; his spirit he exalted because, once freed of its gross partner, it could be lifted above the substantial shows of this earth. Here were combined the Puritan and the Romantic predicament: for the Puritan, and the Christian, a man must be brought low in order that he may rise; he must pass through corruption in order to reach incorruptibility; he must die in the flesh in order to be reborn in the spirit. For the Romantic, the soul, of the artist or perceiver, must first submit to and then transcend the world of "daily solicitude," in Coleridge's apt phrase; it must be humiliated so that it may enlarge; it must suffer so that it may create. The Christian narrative details the record of the fallen, the rescued, and the regenerated soul; the Romantic adventure narrates the inevitable descent and the recovery which bring that moment of ecstatic creative imagination.

Dimmesdale went the Puritan and the Romantic way toward damnation. He ordained his own corruption by convincing himself of his right to put an affront upon nature, his own and "human" nature; he fashioned the split in his own being, and he separated himself from those to whom he was most intimately bound. As he felt the ascent of his mind and the almost excruciating refinement of his soul, he became ever more the victim of the darkening of his consciousness as the implacable ring of fate closed round his whole being. Thus he suffered a double damnation: he died convinced of his moral freedom in a morally predestined world. His sin was hideous, not because of what he did to others—indeed, *The Scarlet Letter* clearly shows how little effect he had on anyone—but because he became that ultimate criminal in Hawthorne's order of humanity, the outcast of the universe.

The Ruined Wall

by Frederick C. Crews

Hester Prynne and Arthur Dimmesdale, in the protective gloom of the forest surrounding Boston, have had their fateful reunion. While little Pearl, sent discreetly out of hearing range, has been romping about in her unrestrained way, the martyred lovers have unburdened themselves. Hester has revealed the identity of Chillingworth and has succeeded in winning Dimmesdale's forgiveness for her previous secrecy. Dimmesdale has explained the agony of his seven years' torment. Self-pity and compassion have led unexpectedly to a revival of desire; "what we did," as Hester boldly remembers, "had a consecration of its own" (I, 195),[1] and Arthur Dimmesdale cannot deny it. In his state of helpless longing he allows himself to be swayed by Hester's insistence that the past can be forgotten, that deep in the wilderness or across the ocean, accompanied and sustained by Hester, he can free himself from the revengeful gaze of Roger Chillingworth.

Hester's argument is of course a superficial one; the ultimate source of Dimmesdale's anguish is not Chillingworth but his own remorse, and this cannot be left behind in Boston. The closing chapters of *The Scarlet Letter* demonstrate this clearly enough, but Hawthorne, with characteristic license, tells us at once that Hester is wrong. "And be the stern and sad truth spoken," he says, "that the breach which guilt has once made into the human soul is never, in this mortal state, repaired. It may be watched and guarded; so that the enemy shall not force his way again into the citadel, and might even, in his subsequent assaults, select some other avenue, in preference to that where he had formerly succeeded. But there is still the ruined wall, and, near it, the stealthy tread of the foe that would win over again his unforgotten triumph" (I, 200f.).

The general drift of this passage is that one must be forever prepared

Reprinted with some revision by Mr. Crews from *The Sins of the Fathers* by Frederick C. Crews. Copyright © 1966 by Frederick C. Crews. Used by permission of the author and Oxford University Press, Inc.

[1] All volume and page references in this essay are to the Ohio State University Press *Centenary Edition*.

for new temptation after a sinful act has been committed. Though this is a religious commonplace, the figure that embodies it bears some interesting implications which may take us into the real tragedy of *The Scarlet Letter*. In the first place, Hawthorne puts no emphasis on the long-term efficacy of a godly will against the enemy's assaults on the citadel of the soul. On the contrary, he seems to write off good intentions as merely the guarding of one breach in the wall, presumably making "some other avenue" of access more available. We are offered, not a religious metaphor of casting out sin, but a psychological metaphor of a desperate and not necessarily successful deployment of defenses. Hawthorne's conception is both mechanistic and fatalistic: a certain force demands entrance, a certain counterforce meets it at the most vulnerable place in the wall, and a possibility is thus envisioned that the assailant force will succeed at some new, undefended point. Even if this too should be prevented, the figure leaves us with a melancholy picture of Man as a creature doomed to be permanently preoccupied with wishes that he finds repugnant.

Anyone who has pondered Hawthorne's finest tales should know that this gloomy determinism was more deeply entrenched in his sense of reality than the moral exhortations he commonly threw against it. Hawthorne's most typical object of interest is a character whose unusual moral sensitivity cannot prevent him from suddenly and permanently falling prey to an obsession with human wickedness—an obsession which springs from a self-repugnance he finds intolerable. The point can be sharpened: Hawthorne's heroes are doomed *by* their moral sensitivity, which seems to boil down to squeamishness rather than virtue. This is where the religious and psychological approaches to criticism, which run parallel in certain respects, must part company abruptly. To qualify as a Christian writer it is necessary to believe that a loathing of one's sinful thoughts is to be cultivated as the first step toward a possible grace. Hawthorne would very much like to believe this, but on the whole he cannot represent it convincingly; his deepest feelings insist that a horror of sin leads not to repentance but to a sickly *modus vivendi* in which sin and the sinner set up mental housekeeping together. It is not a bad rule of thumb, in drawing up a list of Hawthorne's most powerful works, to assume that any story or romance which fails to give this paralyzing vision its due will be slack and insincere.

In this light it is suggestive that the metaphor of the ruined wall seems to identify *guilt* rather than sin or temptation as the soul's chief enemy. To take Hawthorne at his word would be to see Arthur Dimmesdale as chiefly suffering, not from the threat of renewed misconduct, but from morbidity. He can neither accept nor adequately fend off the idea of his guilt, but the idea may infect him through "some other avenue"—perhaps the avenue of unconscious obsession. Hawthorne's little allegory was not designed to bear this much Freudian weight, yet *The Scarlet Letter* as a whole does encourage such a view. Dimmesdale is never in great danger of being mistaken for a passionate love-hero. After his single lapse (his seduction, we might say) he is presented consistently as a moral and physical weakling; indeed, he brings to mind the Victorian notion of the boy who gives all his free time to "self-abuse." We shall see that the comparison is not farfetched. When he does resolve, in the present scene, to make a stab at being a remorseless adulterer, he is able to do so only by humbling himself before Hester in a filial way and borrowing her strength. And, of course, the resolution is pathetically dissipated in a matter of hours.

These considerations undermine the customary view of *The Scarlet Letter* as a fictive illustration of the terrible consequences of sin. We could say with at least equal plausibility that Hawthorne is warning prospective fornicators not to think too precisely on the event. It is not sin, but a revulsion from what was taken to be sin, that sets the chain of "dark necessity" to work; the trouble isn't Dimmesdale's libidinous nature but its weakness before his tyrannous self-accusations and his persistent wish to be holy. This is what locks him together with Chillingworth and Hester in mutual furtiveness. If I were to say in one sentence what *The Scarlet Letter* is "about," I would call it a study in the unconscious interdependence of people who feed off one another's incompleteness in a society which encourages them to dissemble and burn themselves away in secret.

There is another sense in which Hawthorne's main characters are interdependent, not so much in the literal plot as in the authorial mind which grants them existence only as part of a configuration. To someone who has been following Hawthorne's career from a psychological point of view, it is apparent that Chillingworth, Hester, and Dimmesdale stand as father to mother to son, and that Dimmesdale's real crime—meaning his crime in Hawthorne's fantasy—is the perennia Hawthornian one of symbolic incest. The strongest link between *The Scarlet Letter* and the works surrounding it is its devious reference to filial presumption, oppression by an "evil" father-figure whose grotesqueness is a measure of the enmity heaped upon him, and self-immolation before a "good" Father in Heaven. I am not going to pause over the evidence for this reading—a fraction of it can be found in Leslie Fiedler's *Love and Death in the American Novel*—but will concentrate instead on the logic of relationships which are overtly portrayed. It is the distinction of *The Scarlet Letter* that its manifest plot, for the last time in Hawthorne's career, is perfectly coherent without critical recourse to unconscious determination. As in all his finest works, whatever insight we can gain into his private mental drama only helps to deepen, not contradict, the patent emphasis of the story.

Let us return to Dimmesdale in the forest scene, before Hester has gone to work on his misgivings. His nervousness, his mental exhaustion, and his compulsive gesture of placing his hand on his heart reveal a state that we would now call neurotic inhibition. His lack of energy for any of the outward demands of life indicates how all-absorbing is his internal trouble, and the stigma on his chest, though a rather crass piece of symbolism on Hawthorne's part, must also be interpreted psychosomatically. Nor can we avoid observing that Dimmesdale shows the neurotic's reluctance to give up his symptoms. How else can we account for his obtuseness in not having recognized Chillingworth's character? "I might have known it!" he murmurs when Hester forces the revelation upon him. "I did know it! Was not the secret told me in the natural recoil of my heart, at the first sight of him, and as often as I have seen him since? Why did I not understand?" (I, 194) The answer, hidden from Dimmesdale's surface reasoning, is that his relationship with Chillingworth, taken together with the change in mental economy that has accompanied it, has offered perverse satisfactions which he is even now powerless to renounce. Hester, whose will is relatively independent and strong, is the one who makes the decision to break with the past.

We can understand the nature of Dimmesdale's illness by defining the state of mind that has possessed him for seven years. It is of course his concealed act of adultery that lies at the bottom of his self-torment. But why does he lack the courage to make his humiliation public? Dimmesdale himself offers us the clue in a cry of agony: "Of penance I have had enough! Of penitence there has been none! Else, I should long ago have thrown off these garments of mock holiness, and have shown myself to mankind as they will see me at the judgment-seat" (I, 192). The plain meaning of this outburst is that Dimmesdale has never surmounted the libidinal urge that produced his sin. His "penance," including self-flagellation and the more refined torment of submitting to Chillingworth's influence, has failed to purify him because it has been unaccompanied by the feeling of penitence, the resolution to sin no more. Indeed, I submit, Dimmesdale's penance has incorporated and embodied the very urge it has been punishing. If, as he says, he has kept his garments of mock holiness *because* he has not repented, he must mean that in some way or another the forbidden impulse has found gratification in the existing circumstances, in the existing state of his soul. And this state is one of morbid remorse. The stealthy foe has reentered the citadel through the avenue of remorse.

This conclusion may seem less paradoxical if we bear in mind a distinction between remorse and true repentance. In both states the sinful act is condemned morally, but in strict repentance the soul abandons the sin and turns to holier thoughts. Remorse of Dimmesdale's type, on the other hand, is attached to a continual reenacting of the sin in fantasy and hence a continual renewal of the need for self-punishment. Roger Chillingworth, the psychoanalyst *manqué,* understands the process perfectly: "the fear, the remorse, the agony, the ineffectual repentance, the backward rush of sinful thoughts, expelled in vain!" (I, 139) As Hawthorne explains, Dimmesdale's cowardice is the "sister and closely linked companion" (I, 148) of his remorse.

Thus Dimmesdale is helpless to reform himself at this stage because the passional side of his nature has found an outlet, albeit a self-destructive one, in his present miserable situation. The original sexual desire has been granted recognition *on the condition of being punished,* and the punishment itself is a form of gratification. Not only the overt masochism of fasts, vigils, and self-scourging (the last of these makes him laugh, by the way), but also Dimmesdale's emaciation and weariness attest to the spending of his energy against himself. It is important to recognize that this is the same energy previously devoted to passion for Hester. We do not exaggerate the facts of the romance in saying that the question of Dimmesdale's fate, for all its religious context, amounts essentially to the question of what use is to be made of his libido.

We are now prepared to understand the choice that the poor minister faces when Hester holds out the idea of escape. It is not a choice between a totally unattractive life and a happy one (not even Dimmesdale could feel hesitation in that case), but rather a choice of satisfactions, of avenues into the citadel. The seemingly worthless alternative of continuing to admit the morally condemned impulse by the way of remorse has the advantage, appreciated by all neurotics, of preserving the status quo. Still, the other course naturally seems more attractive. If only repression can be weakened—and this is just the task of Hester's rhetoric about freedom—Dimmesdale can hope to return to the previous "breach" of adultery.

In reality, however, these alternatives offer no chance for happiness or even survival. The masochistic course leads straight to death, while the other, which Dimmesdale allows Hester to choose for him, is by now so foreign to his withered, guilt-ridden nature that it can never be put into effect. The resolution to sin will, instead, necessarily redouble the opposing force of conscience, which will be stronger in proportion to the overtness of the libidinal threat. As the concluding chapters of *The Scarlet Letter* prove, the only possible result of Dimmesdale's attempt to impose, in Hawthorne's phrase, "a total change of dynasty and moral code, in that interior kingdom" (I, 217), will be a counterrevolution so violent that it will slay Dimmesdale himself along with his upstart libido. We thus see that in the forest, while Hester is prat-

ing of escape, renewal, and success, Arthur Dimmesdale unknowingly
faces a choice of two paths to suicide.

Now, this psychological impasse is sufficient in itself to refute the
most "liberal" critics of *The Scarlet Letter*—those who take Hester's
proposal of escape as Hawthorne's own advice. However much we may
admire Hester and prefer her boldness to Dimmesdale's self-pity, we
cannot agree that she understands human nature very deeply. Her
shame, despair, and solitude "had made her strong," says Hawthorne,
"but taught her much amiss" (I, 200). What she principally ignores is
the truth embodied in the metaphor of the ruined wall, that men are
altered irreparably by their violations of conscience. Hester herself is
only an apparent exception to this rule. She handles her guilt more
successfully than Dimmesdale because, in the first place, her conscience
is less highly developed than his; and secondly because, as he tells her,
"Heaven hath granted thee an open ignominy, that thereby thou
mayest work out an open triumph over the evil within thee, and the sorrow without" (I, 67). Those who believe that Hawthorne is an ad-
vocate of free love, that adultery has no ill effects on a "normal" nature
like Hester's, have failed to observe that Hester, too, undergoes self-
inflicted punishment. Though permitted to leave, she has remained in
Boston not simply because she wants to be near Arthur Dimmesdale,
but because this has been the scene of her humiliation. "Her sin, her
ignominy, were the roots which she had struck into the soil," says Hawthorne. "The chain that bound her here was of iron links, and galling
to her inmost soul, but never could be broken" (I, 80).

We need not dwell on this argument, for the liberal critics of *The
Scarlet Letter* have been in retreat for many years. Their place has been
taken by subtler readers who say that Hawthorne brings us from sin to
redemption, from materialistic error to pure spiritual truth. The moral
heart of the novel, in this view, is contained in Dimmesdale's Election
Sermon, and Dimmesdale himself is pictured as Christ-like in his holy
death. Hester, in comparison, degenerates spiritually after the first few
chapters; the fact that her thoughts are still on earthly love while
Dimmesdale is looking toward heaven is a serious mark against her.

This redemptive scheme, which rests on the uncriticized assumption
that Hawthorne's point of view is identical with Dimmesdale's at the
end, seems to me to misrepresent the "felt life" of *The Scarlet Letter*
more drastically than the liberal reading. Both take for granted the
erroneous belief that the novel consists essentially of the dramatization
of a moral idea. The tale of human frailty and sorrow, as Hawthorne
calls it in his opening chapter, is treated merely as the fictionalization
of an article of faith. Hawthorne himself, we might observe, did not
share this ability of his critics to shrug off the psychological reality

of his work. *The Scarlet Letter* is, he said, "positively a hell-fired story, into which I found it almost impossible to throw any cheering light."

All parties can agree, in any case, that there is a terrible irony in Dimmesdale's exhilaration when he has resolved to flee with Hester. Being, as Hawthorne describes him, "a true religionist," to whom it would always remain essential "to feel the pressure of a faith about him, supporting, while it confined him within its iron framework" (I, 123), he is ill-prepared to savor his new freedom for what it is. His joy is that of his victorious sexuality, but the release is acknowledged by consciousness only after a significant bowdlerization:

> "Do I feel joy again?" cried he, wondering at himself. "Methought the germ of it was dead in me! O Hester, thou art my better angel! I seem to have flung myself—sick, sin-stained, and sorrow-blackened— down upon these forest leaves, and to have risen up all made anew, and with new powers to glorify Him that hath been merciful! This is already the better life! Why did we not find it sooner?" (I, 201f.)

Hawthorne's portrayal of self-delusion and his compassion are nowhere so powerfully combined as in this passage. The Christian reference to the putting on of the New Man is grimly comic in the light of what has inspired it, but we feel no more urge to laugh at Dimmesdale than we do at Milton's Adam. If in his previous role he has been only, in Hawthorne's phrase, a "subtle, but remorseful hypocrite" (I, 144), here he is striving pathetically to be sincere. His case becomes poignant as we imagine the revenge that his tyrannical conscience must soon take against these new promptings of the flesh. To say merely that Dimmesdale is in a state of theological error is to miss part of the irony; it is precisely his theological loyalty that necessitates his confusion. His sexual nature must be either denied with unconscious sophistry, as in this scene, or rooted out with heroic fanaticism, as in his public confession at the end.

On one point, however, Dimmesdale is not mistaken: he has been blessed with a new energy of body and will. The source of this energy is obviously his libido; he has become physically strong to the degree that he has ceased directing his passion against himself and has attached it to his thoughts of Hester. But as he now returns to town,[2] bent upon renewing his hypocrisy for the four days until the Election Sermon has been given and the ship is to sail, we see that his "cure" has been very incomplete. "At every step he was incited to do some strange, wild, wicked thing or other, with a sense that it would be at

[2] Note, incidentally, the implicit sexuality of his cross-country run, as he "leaped across the plashy places, thrust himself through the clinging underbrush, climbed the ascent, plunged into the hollow . . ." (I, 216).

once involuntary and intentional; in spite of himself, yet growing out of a profounder self than that which opposed the impulse" (I, 217). The minister can scarcely keep from blaspheming to his young and old parishioners as he passes them in the street; he longs to shock a deacon and an old widow with arguments against Christianity, to poison the innocence of a naïve girl who worships him, to teach wicked words to a group of children, and to exchange bawdy jests with a drunken sailor. Here, plainly, is a return of the repressed, and in a form which Freud noted to be typical in severely holy persons.[3] The fact that these impulses have reached the surface of Dimmesdale's mind attests to the weakening of repression in the forest scene, while their perverse and furtive character shows us that repression has not ceased altogether. Hawthorne's own explanation, that Dimmesdale's hidden vices have been awakened because "he had yielded himself *with de-liberate choice,* as he had never done before, to what he *knew* was deadly sin" (I, 222; my italics), gives conscience its proper role as a causative factor. Having left Hester's immediate influence behind in the forest, and having returned to the society where he is thought to be pure, Dimmesdale already finds his "wicked" intentions constrained into the form of a verbal naughtiness which he cannot even bring himself to express.

Now Dimmesdale, presumably after a brief interview with the taunting Mistress Hibbins, arrives at his lodgings. Artfully spurning the attentions of Roger Chillingworth, he eats his supper "with ravenous appetite" (I, 225) and sits down to write the Election Sermon. Without really knowing what words he is setting on paper, and wondering to himself how God could inspire such a sinner as himself, he works all night "with earnest haste and ecstasy" (I, 225). The result is a sermon which, with the addition of spontaneous interpolations in the delivery, will impress its Puritan audience as an epitome of holiness and pathos. Nothing less than the descent of the Holy Ghost will be held sufficient to account for such a performance.

Yet insofar as the Election Sermon will consist of what Dimmesdale has recorded in his siege of possessed writing, we must doubt whether Hawthorne shares the credulous view of the Puritans. Dimmesdale has undergone no discernible change in attitude from the time of his eccentric impulses in the street until the writing of the sermon. Though he works in the room where he has fasted and prayed, and where he can see his old Bible, he is not (as Roy R. Male argues in a chapter of tremulous uplift) sustained by these reminders of his faith. Quite the contrary: he can scarcely believe that he has ever breathed such an atmosphere. "But he seemed to stand apart, and eye this former self

[3] See, for example, *Collected Papers,* III, 331, 599f.

with scornful, pitying, but half-envious curiosity. That self was gone! Another man had returned out of the forest; a wiser one; with a knowledge of hidden mysteries which the simplicity of the former never could have reached" (I, 223). In short, the Election Sermon is written by the same man who wants to corrupt young girls in the street, and the same newly liberated sexuality "inspires" him in both cases. If the written form of the Election Sermon *is* a great Christian document, as we have no reason to doubt, this is attributable not to Dimmesdale's holiness but to his libido, which gives him creative strength and an intimate acquaintance with the reality of sin. Only by appealing to classic psychoanalytic theory can we appreciate Hawthorne's astonishing brilliance in sending Dimmesdale without hesitation from the greatest blasphemy to fervent religious rhetoric.

There is little doubt that Dimmesdale has somehow recovered his piety in the three days that intervene between the writing of the sermon and its delivery. Both Hester and Mistress Hibbins "find it hard to believe him the same man" (I, 241) who emerged from the forest. Though he is preoccupied with his imminent sermon as he marches past Hester, his energy seems greater than ever and his nervous mannerism is absent. We could say, if we liked, that at this point God's grace has already begun to sustain Dimmesdale, but there is nothing in Hawthorne's description to warrant a resort to supernatural explanations. It seems likely that Dimmesdale has by now felt the full weight of his conscience's case against adultery, has already determined to confess his previous sin publicly, and so is no longer suffering from repression. His sexual energy is now free, not to attach itself to Hester, but to be sublimated into the passion of delivering his sermon and then expelled forever.

The ironies in Dimmesdale's situation as he leaves the church, having preached with magnificent power, are extremely subtle. His career, as Hawthorne tells us, has touched the proudest eminence that any clergyman could hope to attain, yet this eminence is due, among other things, to "a reputation of whitest sanctity" (I, 249). Furthermore, Hester has been silently tormented by an inquisitive mob while Dimmesdale has been preaching, and we feel the injustice of the contrast. And yet Dimmesdale has already made the choice that will render him worthy of the praise he is now receiving. If his public hypocrisy has not yet been dissolved, his hypocrisy with himself is over. It would be small-minded not to recognize that Dimmesdale has, after all, achieved a point of heroic independence—an independence not only of his fawning congregation but also of Hester, who frankly resents it. If the Christian reading of *The Scarlet Letter* judges Hester too roughly on theological grounds, it is at least correct in seeing that she lacks the detachment to appreciate Dimmesdale's final act of courage. While she remains on the steady level of her womanly affections, Dimmesdale, who has previously stooped below his ordinary manhood, is now ready to act with the exalted fervor of a saint.

All the moral ambiguity of *The Scarlet Letter* makes itself felt in Dimmesdale's moment of confession. We may truly say that no one has a total view of what is happening. The citizens of Boston, for whom it would be an irreverent thought to connect their minister with Hester, turn to various rationalizations to avoid comprehending the scene. Hester is bewildered, and Pearl feels only a generalized sense of grief. But what about Arthur Dimmesdale? Is he really on his way to heaven as he proclaims God's mercy in his dying words?

> "He hath proved his mercy, most of all, in my afflictions. By giving me this burning torture to bear upon my breast! By sending yonder dark and terrible old man, to keep the torture always at red-heat! By bringing me hither, to die this death of triumphant ignominy before the people! Had either of these agonies been wanting, I had been lost for ever! Praised be his name! His will be done! Farewell!" (I, 256f.)

This reasoning, which sounds so cruel to the ear of rational humanism, has the logic of Christian doctrine behind it; it rests on the paradox that a man must lose his life to save it. The question that the neo-orthodox interpreters of *The Scarlet Letter* invariably ignore, however, is whether Hawthorne has prepared us to understand this scene only in doctrinal terms. Has he abandoned his usual irony and lost himself in religious transport?

The question ultimately amounts to a matter of critical method: whether we are to take the action of *The Scarlet Letter* in natural or supernatural terms. Hawthorne offers us naturalistic explanations for everything that happens, and though he also puts forth opposite theories—Pearl is an elf-child, Mistress Hibbins is a witch, and so on—this mode of thinking is discredited by the simplicity of the people who employ it. We cannot conscientiously say that Chillingworth *is* a devil, for example, when Hawthorne takes such care to show us how his devilishness has proceeded from his physical deformity, his sense of inferiority and impotence, his sexual jealousy, and his perverted craving for knowledge. Hawthorne carries symbolism to the border of allegory but does not cross over. As for Dimmesdale's retrospective idea that God's mercy has been responsible for the whole course of events, we cannot absolutely deny that this may be true; but we can remark that if it *is* true, Hawthorne has vitiated his otherwise brilliant study of motivation.

Nothing in Dimmesdale's behavior on the scaffold is incongruous with his psychology as we first examined it in the forest scene. We merely find ourselves at the conclusion to the breakdown of repression that began there, and which has necessarily brought about a renewal of opposition to the forbidden impulses. Dimmesdale has been heroic in choosing to eradicate his libidinal self with one stroke, but his heroism follows a sound principle of mental economy. Further repression, which is the only other alternative for his conscience-ridden nature, would only lead to a slower and more painful death through masochistic remorse. Nor can we help but see that his confession passes beyond a humble admission of sinfulness and touches the pathological. His stigma has become the central object in the universe: "God's eye beheld it! The angels were for ever pointing at it! The Devil knew it well, and fretted it continually with the touch of his burning finger!" (I, 255) Dimmesdale is so obsessed with his own guilt that he negates the Christian dogma of original sin: "behold me here, the one sinner of the world!" (I, 254) This strain of egoism in his "triumphant ignominy" does not subtract from his courage, but it casts doubt on his theory that all the preceding action has been staged by God for the purpose of saving his soul.

However much we may admire Dimmesdale's final asceticism, there are no grounds for taking it as Hawthorne's moral ideal. The last developments of plot in *The Scarlet Letter* approach the "mythic level" which redemption-minded critics love to discover, but the myth is wholly secular and worldly. Pearl, who has hitherto been a "messenger of anguish" to her mother, is emotionally transformed as she kisses Dimmesdale on the scaffold. "A spell was broken. The great scene of grief, in which the wild infant bore a part, had developed all her sympathies; and as her tears fell upon her father's cheek, they were the pledge that she would grow up amid human joy and sorrow, nor for ever do battle with the world, but be a woman in it" (I, 256). Thanks to Chillingworth's bequest—for Chillingworth, too, finds that a spell is broken when Dimmesdale confesses, and he is capable of at least one generous act before he dies—Pearl is made "the richest heiress of her day, in the New World" (I, 261). At last report she has become the wife of a European nobleman and is living very happily across the sea. This grandiose and perhaps slightly whimsical epilogue has one undeniable effect on the reader: it takes him as far as possible from the scene and spirit of Dimmesdale's farewell. Pearl's immense wealth, her noble title, her lavish and impractical gifts to Hester, and of course her successful escape from Boston all serve to disparage the Puritan sense of reality. From this distance we look back to Dimmesdale's egocentric confession, not as a moral example which Hawthorne would like us to follow, but as the last link in a chain of compulsion that has now been relaxed.

To counterbalance this impression we have the case of Hester, for whom the drama on the scaffold can never be completely over. After raising Pearl in a more generous atmosphere she voluntarily returns to Boston to resume, or rather to begin, her state of penitence. We must note, however, that this penitence seems to be devoid of theological content; Hester has returned because Boston and the scarlet letter offer her "a more real life" (I, 262) than she could find elsewhere, even with Pearl. This simply confirms Hawthorne's emphasis on the irrevocability of guilty acts. And though Hester is now selfless and humble, it is not because she believes in Christian submissiveness but because all passion has been spent. To the women who seek her help "in the continually recurring trials of wounded, wasted, wronged, misplaced, or erring and sinful passion" (I, 263), Hester does not disguise her conviction that women are pathetically misunderstood in her society. She assures her wretched friends that at some later period "a new truth would be revealed, in order to establish the whole relation between man and woman on a surer ground of mutual happiness" (I, 263). Hawthorne may or may not believe the prediction, but it has a retrospective importance in *The Scarlet Letter*. Hawthorne's characters originally acted in ignorance of passion's strength and persistence, and so they became its slaves.

"It is a curious subject of observation and inquiry," says Hawthorne at the end, "whether hatred and love be not the same thing at bottom. Each, in its utmost development, supposes a high degree of intimacy and heart-knowledge; each renders one individual dependent for the food of his affections and spiritual life upon another; each leaves the passionate lover, or the no less passionate hater, forlorn and desolate by the withdrawal of his object" (I, 260). These penetrating words remind us that the tragedy of *The Scarlet Letter* has chiefly sprung, not from Puritan society's imposition of false social ideals on the three main characters, but from their own inner world of frustrated desires. Hester, Dimmesdale, and Chillingworth have been ruled by feelings only half perceived, much less understood and regulated by consciousness; and these feelings, as Hawthorne's bold equation of love and hatred implies, successfully resist translation into terms of good and evil. Hawthorne does not leave us simply with the Sunday-school lesson that we should "be true" (I, 260), but with a tale of passion through which we glimpse the ruined wall—the terrible certainty that, as Freud put it, the ego is not master in its own house. It is this intuition that enables Hawthorne to reach a tragic vision worthy of the name: to see to the bottom of his created characters, to understand the inner necessity of everything they do, and thus to pity and forgive them in the very act of laying bare their weaknesses.

Form and Content
in *The Scarlet Letter*

by John C. Gerber

Content in *The Scarlet Letter* consists of those three matters which dominate the thoughts and actions of the characters: sin, isolation, and reunion. Generally speaking, with Hawthorne isolation is inevitably the result of sin, and the desire for reunion is usually the result of isolation. But it is a mistake to suppose that any one of these terms can be employed successfully in a general sense. No one of them is constant in meaning throughout the book.

There is, for example, no such thing as uniformity in the concept of sin.[1] To assume this is to confuse the characters and to misinterpret most of the important speeches. Sin in *The Scarlet Letter* is a violation of only that which the sinner *thinks* he violates. To one character, adultery is transgression against God's law, to another, no more than a violation of the natural order of things. Likewise, to one character hypocrisy is a violation of his own nature, to another, a transgression against the moral code of the community. To speak, therefore, even of adultery or hypocrisy without discovering what they mean to each individual is to become hopelessly confused about what Hawthorne is doing. Furthermore, as the nature of the sin differs, so must the nature of the isolation which is its result.

More than anything else, probably, *The Scarlet Letter* is a study of isolation.[2] And just as one cannot generalize about sin in the book, so

---

"Form and Content in The Scarlet Letter," *by John C. Gerber.* New England Quarterly, *XVII (March 1944), 26-28, 29-34. Copyright 1944 by the New England Quarterly. Reprinted by permission of the New England Quarterly and John C. Gerber.*

[1] Clarence Faust was the first to suggest this point to me. I am grateful for other insights to Gordon Roper and Walter Blair.

[2] Mr. Paul Elmer More makes this even more emphatic in "The Solitude of Nathaniel Hawthorne," *Shelburne Essays,* First Series (New York, 1904), p. 33: "From the opening scene at the prison door, which, 'like all that pertains to crime, seemed never to have known a youthful era,' to the final scene on the scaffold, where the tragic imagination of the author speaks with a power barely surpassed in the books of the world, the whole plot of the romance moves about this one conception of our human isolation as the penalty of transgression."

is it impossible to speak of isolation as though it were always one and the same thing. When a character feels isolated, he feels isolated from someone or something. Isolation, therefore, is a feeling of estrangement from those persons or elements whose code the individual feels that he has violated. By this definition, the study of isolation in *The Scarlet Letter* becomes a matter not only of comparing characters but also of ascertaining the successive degrees of estrangement within a single character.

The problem of reunion is even more complex. Given a sinful act, the consequent chain of cause and effect is something like this: sin brings isolation, isolation creates suffering, and suffering brings the desire to alleviate one's condition through reunion with the element from which one is isolated. At this point, however, an interesting paradox becomes apparent. Reunion in *The Scarlet Letter* is at once both highly individualized and strictly conventionalized. It is individualized in the sense that a character's attempts at reunion are obviously the result of his particular sense of sin and isolation; it is conventionalized in that Hawthorne allows only one pattern for its successful accomplishment. This pattern has three components: a personal sense of responsibility, repentance, and penance. The first of these is essential to the second and third but does not necessarily create them, as Dimmesdale's suffering bears witness. The second is of supreme importance but seldom occurs. In *The Scarlet Letter* there are only three examples of repentance, of which only the least important is presented in detail. The third, penance, is voluntary action designed totally to expiate the wrong. As such, it is not to be confused with the false type of penance which exists apart from repentance and which is wholly ineffectual. True penance must follow and be a manifestation of inward repentance. Ordinarily, it involves both confession and a plea for forgiveness. These, then, are the terms of reunion; and though isolation inevitably follows sin, reunion dispels isolation only when these terms are met.[3] . . .

[3] It must be conceded immediately that these terms do not constitute a process which fully reestablishes the original union. Reunion is not Christian salvation, and the two terms should not be used interchangeably. Indeed, Dimmesdale in his dying moment warns that it is vain to hope to meet even in the hereafter in "an everlasting and pure reunion." It is such a statement that gives support to Mr. Woodberry's assertion in *Nathaniel Hawthorne* (Boston, 1902), p. 193, that "the idea of salvation, of healing, is but little present and is not felt." To this, Mr. Austin Warren, in *Nathaniel Hawthorne* (New York, 1934), p. xl, adds: "Certainly Hawthorne has no hope in his creative mind. This is a sorry world; but we can really do nothing about it. Men necessarily sin; but they must be held strictly accountable for their sins all the same. They must repent, but repentance cannot raise the fallen." These gloomy aspects to the story, however, should not blind one to the fact that reunion constitutes a major theme, and that though it does not bring the

No one of the three main characters comes into the story guiltless. Of the three, however, Hester has the misfortune of being the only one unable to hide her guilt, and so it is upon her that the penalties of the community fall. It is unnecessary to go into detail about her public humiliation or her subsequent life in the small cottage at the edge of town. What interests us is the reaction which this enforced estrangement has upon her. And to understand this, we must first understand Hester's own attitude toward her misstep.

In the first place, it is evident that Hester does not feel that she has sinned against God. Partly this is so because God has never been a very real presence in her life. But chiefly, we are led to infer, it is because she experiences no new sense of estrangement from Him as the result of her adultery. She attends church "trusting to share the Sabbath smile of the Universal father" and undoubtedly would do so were the minister able to refrain from making her the topic of his sermon. Moreover, though man has punished her for her sin, God has given her "a lovely child, whose place was on that same dishonored bosom, to connect her parent for ever with the race and descent of mortals, and to be finally a blessed soul in heaven!" God, then, has not looked with unkindness upon her deed.

Hester is certain, too, that she has violated no law of her own nature. She is by nature affectionate, even passionate. Her relation with Dimmesdale, consequently, has been the almost inescapable result of her own nature, not a violation of it. As a matter of fact, it is this same affection which now holds her to Boston, even though she concocts for her conscience a pleasantly moral half-truth that she is remaining in order to effect a purification of her soul. Hawthorne does not make all of this completely clear in the first eight chapters. But later, when Hester speaks of her deed as having a "consecration of its own," we can see how firmly she believes that her own nature and the deed have been in harmony.

In the third place, it is plain that Hester does not feel that she has sinned against the community. Indeed, from the very beginning it is evident that the selectmen's attempt to induce inward repentance by outward penance is to result in failure. For though Hester submits to the public exhibition and to the wearing of the scarlet letter, it is clear that her heart has not been touched. Even her dress on that first day seems to express "the desperate recklessness of her mood." With the passing of time, she tones down her dress and softens her attitude, but she continues to manifest rebellion in the bright and imaginative embroidery of the letter which the community intended as a heavy sign

---

joy of Christian salvation it does bring relief from suffering in those instances when it is achieved.

of guilt. Pearl, the other symbol of her error, she clothes in the gayest
of colors. If any further evidence is needed, it is contained in the statement that she "was patient,—a martyr, indeed,—but she forebore to
pray for her enemies; lest, in spite of her forgiving aspirations, the
words of the blessing should stubbornly twist themselves into a curse."
The plain truth of the matter is that Hester feels she has not sinned
against the community, and therefore that the community has no right
to inflict penalties. The only real result, then, of the community's action is to isolate Hester from her neighbors in spirit as well as in
person.

Yet in spite of all this, Hester knows that her deed has been wrong
and that, somehow, the result cannot be good. This is manifest in her
anxiety for Pearl, whom she watches constantly, fearful of detecting
some "dark and wild peculiarity." Soon she finds it in Pearl's way-
wardness and unpredictability.

> The child could not be made amendable to rules. In giving her exis-
> tence, a great law had been broken; and the result was a being whose
> elements were perhaps beautiful and brilliant, but all in disorder; or
> with an order peculiar to themselves, amidst which the point of variety
> and arrangement was difficult or impossible to be discovered.

The great law which Hester feels she has broken, therefore, is the law
of order. Not conscious of being a sinner in the orthodox sense of the
word, she is nevertheless bitterly aware of the fact that she and
Dimmesdale have introduced an act of disorder into an orderly universe. And being aware of this, she can realize that some estrangement
from the natural course of life is her due. That this estrangement
should be forcibly meted out by the community, however, she can
logically resent as being cruelly irrelevant.

The first act of the community with regard to Hester is a distinct
failure. Its second is just as wide of the mark when, in an attempt to
bring some peace to her spirit after her ordeal in the market-place, it
makes future peace almost unattainable. For by introducing Chillingworth into her prison apartment, the community through its jailer can
be held at least indirectly responsible for the vow of secrecy which
Chillingworth is enabled to extract. By natural inclination, Hester
scorns deception. Consequently, to have become partner to a plot
which surrenders her lover to his worst enemy is for her to commit an
act which ultimately she regards as an inexcusable violation of her
nature.[4] The immediate result, of course, is to place an additional

---

[4] To avoid confusion, it is necessary to keep in mind that "nature" as applied
by Hawthorne to a character's essential constitution refers to the original constitution which the character possesses before sin or circumstance warps it. For
Hester to be true to her nature is for her to look, to feel, and to think in harmony

barrier between her and Dimmesdale; the ultimate result is to create that remorse which is a sign of division and estrangement within the soul.

Like Hester, Chillingworth does not come into the market-place of Boston guiltless. Formerly a brilliant and even kindly man, he erred first when he prevailed upon Hester to marry him. The nature of this act is plain to him. "Mine was the first wrong," he admits, "when I betrayed thy budding youth into a false and unnatural relation with my decay." With sure insight he is quick to see that out of this violation of the natural order only further falsity can result. "Nay, from the moment when we came down the old church steps together, a married pair, I might have beheld the bale-fire of that scarlet letter blazing at the end of our path!" But having admitted this responsibility, Chillingworth is unable or unwilling to go further.

Given the opportunity through the community's manipulation of events, Chillingworth chooses to intensify rather than to expiate his guilt. Hester he simply decides to ignore, and in so doing he sins again by setting up a relation which he, if forced, would have to admit to be false to his marriage vows and unnatural to human affection. To assert to Hester that "between thee and me, the scale hangs fairly balanced" is simply to deny the responsibility which he professed a moment before. One sin in Hawthorne's scheme never checks off another. Hester's lover, moreover, Chillingworth vows to have for himself. To achieve this, he must conceal his identity and thereby set up a false relation between himself and the community. In this fashion he prepares the ground for the "black flower" which is to be his third and greatest sin.

Dimmesdale is not a central figure in the first part of *The Scarlet Letter;* yet the effect of the community upon him is easily discernible and none the less profound. From the first it is obvious that Dimmesdale is a godly person. To his fellow townsmen he is their "godly pastor" or the "godly Master Dimmesdale." It is emphasized, moreover, that "so far as his duties would permit, he trod in the shadowy by-

---

with her original attributes: her feminine, almost voluptuous, appearance, her warmly personal affection, and her scrupulous regard for simple truthfulness. None of her later attributes are ever characterized as "natural": her colorless, statuelike appearance, her self-effacing benevolence, her radical speculation. These, according to Hawthorne, are the result of her innate tenderness' being so deeply crushed into her heart that only some "magic" can effect a transformation, i.e., a return to the "natural." The same principle operates with respect to Dimmesdale and Chillingworth. When Hawthorne speaks of the "constitution of his nature" he is referring to Dimmesdale's original nature, in which human affection and timidity are the dominant emotions, and truthfulness, as refined by Calvinistic theology, the dominant trait of his thinking. And, as pointed out later, Chillingworth by "nature" is gifted with kindness and a rigorous scientific integrity.

paths, and thus kept himself simple and child-like; coming forth, when occasion was, with a freshness, and fragrance, and dewy purity of thought, which, as many people said, affected them like the speech of an angel." It is not surprising, consequently, that when Dimmesdale finally comes to confess his act of adultery, he should consider it a violation of God's laws. This is, of course, anticipating a later part of the book, but the point to be made here is that when we first see Dimmesdale, we see a man already conscious of having sinned against his Lord. The resulting estrangement has already made its mark upon him.

Unfortunately for Dimmesdale, his sin cannot remain uncomplicated so long as he remains in Boston. For the righteous colony of Massachusetts is a place "where iniquity is dragged out into the sunshine." To hide one's sin is to violate the basic principle of the community's moral code. Thus is a new issue raised for the unhappy minister. To refrain from confessing his adultery is to add sin against the community to sin against God. The issue, in fact, is more than raised; it is forced home. In view of the entire town he is compelled by the Reverend Mr. Wilson to exhort Hester to reveal the identity of the baby's father. Thus, before the whole community, by failing to confess his guilt Dimmesdale breaks the community's cardinal precept. Like Hester and Chillingworth, he becomes twice the sinner and twice the outcast. This is a sorry result, indeed, for the activities of so godly a place as Boston in the seventeenth century!

The Scarlet Letter
as a Love Story

by Ernest Sandeen

The Scarlet Letter has been interpreted as a story of sins and sinners for so long that this perspective has hardened into a convention. In Hester, Dimmesdale, and Pearl the sin of adultery and its consequences are seen; to Dimmesdale is added the further, less sympathetic sin of hypocrisy; and beyond the pale stands Chillingworth in his isolating sin of pride and self-consuming revenge. Once this standard point of view is assumed, it can be supported by what is incontrovertibly in the text, but if the angle of attention is shifted so that the novel is seen as a love story, that is, as a tragedy of the grand passion rather than as a tale of sinful passion, then certain features in our picture of the novel, obscure before, will leap into prominence and some of the previously more emphatic features will change their value in relation to the whole composition. Hawthorne's masterpiece may remain for us a haunted book, but it will be haunted by a mystery which we can identify as the mystery of erotic passion itself. It will be seen, in this perspective, that passion is the fixed reality throughout the novel and that it is "sin" which is the shifting, ambiguous term, as it is refracted in the many-sided ironies of the plot and of the narrative commentary. Further, from this point of view it becomes clear that the passion of the lovers is entering its most interesting phase when the story opens instead of being over and done with, except for its consequences, as is tacitly assumed in the conventional approach.

The more extreme and sentimental postures of "courtly love" do not appear in *The Scarlet Letter* since the setting, after all, is seventeenth century Boston. Yet the initial situation involving a husband, his wife, and her lover is obviously "classic." Whenever marriage and passion come into conflict in the typical love story of our Western tra-

Reprinted by permission of the Modern Language Association from "The Scarlet Letter *as a Love Story*," *by Ernest Sandeen.* Publications of the Modern Language Association, *LXXVII (September 1962), 425. Copyright © 1962 by the Modern Language Association.*

dition—and they usually do—the claims of passion far outshine those of its humbler rival. Hester's marriage, in conformity with the tradition, is poor and mean compared to her love affair. In the prison interview Hester reminds her husband that from the first she had "felt no love, nor feigned any." Chillingworth, on his part, admits that he had married Hester simply because he had wished to kindle "a household fire" for his later years.

Far different from this passionless domestic arrangement is the love which unites Hester and Arthur. Although it is disastrous in that it wrecks all possibilities for happiness in their lives, it matures them morally and spiritually; under its influence they grow to a tragic height of character which they otherwise would probably not have reached. Yet the passion which works for their moral development is erotic and adulterous—a paradox which characterizes and might even be said to define the Western "heresy" of love.

Finally, however, it must be emphasized that Hawthorne in *The Scarlet Letter* was writing his own version of the traditional story of passion. In fact the patent features of the archetype which appear in the novel make his departure from the tradition appear all the more radical and dramatic.

From "Achievement and Frustration"

by Leslie A. Fiedler

In the seeming Eden of the New World, a man and woman, who are still essentially the old Adam and Eve, deceive themselves for a moment into believing that they can escape the consequences of sin. The woman has served a prison term and bears on her breast the sign of her shame, and the man, who was the occasion of that shame, has lived secretly with his guilt and powerless remorse; yet in their deluded hope, they meet in the forest, plot a flight from the world of law and religion. For an instant, that hope seems to transfigure not only them, but the dark wood into which they have strayed. When Hester flings aside the scarlet letter and lets down her hair, the forest glows to life: "Such was the sympathy of . . . wild, heathen Nature . . . never subjugated by law, nor illumined by higher truth with the bliss of these two spirits. Love . . . must always create a sunshine that overflows upon the natural world."

Yet Hawthorne cannot grant these lovers even the mitigated bliss he earlier permitted the May King and Queen in "The Maypole of Merry Mount"; for between them lies the taboo of adultery, as real to him as to his ancestors. Hawthorne does not accept without qualification the judgment of his ancestors, though he condemns Hester's proposal of flight even as they would have and uses to describe it the Faustian metaphor. He is, after all, a modern, secular thinker, for whom nothing is self-evident, everything problematical; and he is being tempted as he writes to make a retreat from his own community very like Hester's. Yet, for all his quarrel with Puritanism and its persecuting zeal, he knows that no American can really leave behind the America which the Puritans have once and for all defined.

America represents for Hawthorne not only the marginal settlement,

From Part Two "Achievement and Frustration" in Love and Death in the American Novel *by Leslie A. Fiedler. New York: Dell, 1966, pp. 233-34. Copyright © 1966 by Leslie A. Fiedler. Reprinted by permission of Stein and Day, Inc., Jonathan Cape, Ltd., and Leslie A. Fiedler.*

set between corrupt civilization and unredeemed nature, but also the rule of moral law in the place of self-justifying passion or cynical gallantry. In *The Scarlet Letter,* passion justifies nothing, while its denial redeems all. The fallen Eden of this world remains fallen; but the sinful priest purges himself by public confession, becomes worthy of his sole remaining way to salvation, death. Even Hester, though sin and suffering have made her an almost magical figure, a polluted but still terrible goddess, must finally accept loneliness and self-restraint instead of the love and freedom she dreamed. She cannot become the greater Ann Hutchinson she might have been had she remained unfallen, cannot redeem her sex from the indignities against which she once raged and plotted in secret. Passion has opened up for her no new possibilities, only closed off older ones.

Chronology of Important Dates

1804   Nathaniel Hawthorne born July 4 in Salem, Massachusetts.

Thomas Jefferson elected President for a second term.

1808   Father, a sea captain, died in Surinam, New Guinea.

James Madison elected President; importation of slaves prohibited.

1821-25   Attended Bowdoin College.

1821, James Monroe assumed Presidency for a second term; 1823, Monroe Doctrine.

1825-37   Read and trained himself as a writer while living in the "chamber under the eaves" in his mother's house, Salem.

J. Q. Adams, Jackson, and Van Buren served as Presidents; 1830, Webster-Hayne debate over state sovereignty; 1832, nullification controversy; 1836, Republic of Texas established.

1828   Published *Fanshawe* anonymously.

Andrew Jackson elected President.

1837   Published the first edition of *Twice-Told Tales*.

Financial panic.

1839-40   Worked as Measurer in the Boston Custom House.

1840, William Henry Harrison elected President.

1841   Lived at Brook Farm at West Roxbury, Mass., April to November.

First covered wagon train arrived in California via the Oregon Trail.

1842   Married Sophia Peabody.

Webster-Ashburton treaty settled boundary between Maine and New Brunswick.

1844   Daughter Una born.

First telegraph message sent by Samuel F. B. Morse; Texas

Hawthorne   *Historical Events*

		annexation treaty signed; James K. Polk elected President.
1846-49	Worked as Surveyor in the Salem Custom House.	1846, war with Mexico; settlement of Oregon boundary; 1848, discovery of gold in California; Taylor elected President.
1850	Published *The Scarlet Letter*; moved to a farm near Lenox in the Berkshires.	Compromise of 1850; President Taylor died, succeeded by Millard Fillmore.
1851	Published *The House of the Seven Gables, The Snow Image and Other Twice-Told Tales,* and *True Stories from History and Biography*; daughter Rose born; moved to West Newton, near Boston.	
1852	Published *The Blithedale Romance, A Wonder-Book for Girls and Boys,* and a campaign biography of Franklin Pierce.	Franklin Pierce, Hawthorne's friend, elected President; *Uncle Tom's Cabin* published in book form.
1853-57	Served as United States Consul in Liverpool.	1854, Kansas-Nebraska bill passed; 1856, James Buchanan elected President.
1857-59	Lived in Rome and Florence and at Redcar, England.	1857, Dred Scott decision; financial panic; 1858, Lincoln-Douglas debates; 1859, John Brown's raid on Harpers Ferry.
1860	Published *The Marble Faun*; returned to the Wayside in Concord, Mass.	Lincoln elected President.
1863	Published *Our Old Home*.	Emancipation Proclamation; battles of Vicksburg and Gettysburg.
1864	Died May 19 at Plymouth, New Hampshire; buried May 23 in Sleepy Hollow Cemetery, Concord.	Lincoln reelected; Sherman's march through Georgia.

Notes on the Editor and Contributors

JOHN C. GERBER is Chairman of the Department of English and Director of the School of Letters at the University of Iowa. He is chairman of the editorial board for the new Iowa-California edition of the works of Mark Twain.

FREDERICK C. CREWS teaches at the University of California at Berkeley. In addition to *Sins of the Fathers: Hawthorne's Psychological Themes* (1966) he has written *Tragedy of Manners; Moral Drama in the Later Novels of Henry James* (1957), *E. M. Forster: The Perils of Humanism* (1962), and the enormously witty *The Pooh Perplex* (1963), in which he burlesques the leading schools of criticism.

EDWARD H. DAVIDSON is Professor of English at the University of Illinois. His best known work on Hawthorne is *Hawthorne's Last Phase* (1949, 1967).

RICHARD HARTER FOGLE, Professor of English at the University of North Carolina, has written notably on Coleridge, Keats, and Shelley and is the author of *Hawthorne's Fiction: The Light and the Dark* (1952).

HUGH N. MACLEAN is Professor and Chairman of the Department of English of the State University of New York at Albany. He is author of *The Critical Reader* (1962).

F. O. MATTHIESSEN was Professor of English at Harvard at the time of his death in 1950. In addition to his great critical work entitled *The American Renaissance* (1941) he wrote extensively on T. S. Eliot, Henry James, Sarah Orne Jewett, and Theodore Dreiser.

DONALD A. RINGE teaches American literature at the University of Kentucky. He has published critical biographies of James Fenimore Cooper (1962) and Charles Brockden Brown (1964).

GORDON ROPER is Professor of English at Trinity College of the University of Toronto. He has published extensively on Hawthorne, Melville, and Canadian fiction.

CHARLES RYSKAMP teaches at Princeton. In addition to Hawthorne he has written about such literary figures as William Cowper, James Boswell, and Oscar Wilde.

ERNEST SANDEEN is Professor and Chairman of the Department of English at the University of Notre Dame. He is the author of a volume of poetry,

Antennas of Silence (1953), and has contributed to *Fifty Years of the American Novel* (1951) and *American Classics Reconsidered* (1958).

LELAND SCHUBERT after retiring from teaching at Madison College has been a braillist in Cleveland, Ohio, making books on order for the blind.

JOSEPH SCHWARTZ is Professor and Chairman of the Department of English at Marquette University. He has written *Perspectives on Language* and has been a coeditor of *A Reader for Writers* and *The Province of Rhetoric* (1965).

WILLIAM BYSSHE STEIN teaches at the State University of New York at Binghamton. He has written on Emerson, Thoreau, and Stephen Crane as well as producing *Hawthorne's Faust* (1953).

HYATT H. WAGGONER is Professor of English at Brown University. His books include *The Heel of Elohim: Science and Values in Modern American Poetry* (1950), *Hawthorne, A Critical Study* (1955), and *William Faulkner: From Jefferson to the World* (1959).

CHARLES CHILD WALCUTT teaches at Queens College. He divides his scholarly interests between basic reading and American literature, his best known works in the latter field being *American Literary Naturalism: A Divided Stream* (1956), *An Anatomy of Prose* (1962), *Jack London* (1966), and *Man's Changing Mask: Modes and Methods of Characterization in Fiction* (1966).

Selected Bibliography

Darrel Abel, "Hawthorne's Hester," *College English*, XIII (1952), 303-9. In the story of Hester Prynne Hawthorne exhibits the appeal and yet the inadequacy of romantic individualism.

Walter Blair, "Color, Light, and Shadow in Hawthorne's Fiction," *New England Quarterly*, XV (1942), 74-94. The symbolic use of color, light, and shadow in *The Scarlet Letter* helps to reveal the moral conditions of the four main characters.

Neal F. Doubleday, "Hawthorne's Hester and Feminism," *PMLA*, LIV (1939), 825-28. As exhibited in Hester, feminism for Hawthorne is the result of estrangement from the normal life of woman.

Chester E. Eisinger, "Pearl and the Puritan Heritage," *College English*, XII (1951), 323-29. Pearl, who is a lost soul because her master is not God but nature, is released from the thralldom of nature and humanized by Dimmesdale's regeneration.

Charles Feidelson, Jr., *"The Scarlet Letter," Hawthorne Centenary Essays*, ed. Roy Harvey Pearce. Columbus: Ohio State University Press, 1964. Although *The Scarlet Letter* is a moral tale in a Christian setting, its imaginative method is distinctly historical; the book is "not only *about* but also *written out* of a felt historical situation."

James D. Hart, *"The Scarlet Letter*: One Hundred Years After," *New England Quarterly*, XXIII (1950), 381-95. In the romance that best exhibits his response to his moral dilemma as artist, Hawthorne draws his characters as different sides of his own personality.

Hubert H. Hoeltje, "The Writing of *The Scarlet Letter*," *New England Quarterly*, XXVII (1954), 326-46. The most detailed account of Hawthorne's life just before and during the composition of the romance.

Q. D. Leavis, "Hawthorne as Poet," *Sewanee Review*, LIX (1951), 179-205, 426-58. A careful analysis of Hawthorne's works shows that he was an original artist as well as a creator of a literary tradition.

Mark Van Doren, *"The Scarlet Letter," Nathaniel Hawthorne*. New York: William Sloane Associates, 1949. The greatness of *The Scarlet Letter* lies in the fact that the characters, notably Hester, are neither cold nor empty;

though abstractions in a sense, they nevertheless operate as personalities and determine the plot.

Larzer Ziff, "The Ethical Dimension of 'The Custom House,'" *Modern Language Notes,* LXXIII (1958), 338-44. Hawthorne professed to be disappointed with *The Scarlet Letter* in "The Custom House" because he thought it too complete an escape into the past and the imaginary, too little concerned with the material and the actual.

See also the works listed in the footnotes to the Introduction.